EAST LOTHIAN
FOLK
TALES

EAST LOTHIAN
FOLK
TALES

TIM PORTEUS

ILLUSTRATED BY MAGS MACFARLANE

FOREWORD BY DONALD SMITH

The
History
Press

First published 2017

The History Press
The Mill, Brimscombe Port
Stroud, Gloucestershire, GL5 2QG
www.thehistorypress.co.uk

Text © Tim Porteus, 2017
Illustrations © Mags Macfarlane, 2017

The right of Tim Porteus to be identified as the Author
of this work has been asserted in accordance with the
Copyright, Designs and Patents Act 1988.

British Library Cataloguing in Publication Data.
A catalogue record for this book is available from the British Library.

ISBN 978 0 7509 8004 3

Typesetting and origination by The History Press
Printed and bound by CPI Group (UK) Ltd, Croydon, CR04 YY

CONTENTS

ABOUT THE AUTHOR

TIM PORTEUS is a professional storyteller who uses traditional folklore and local historical tales to connect people, and enhance a sense of place and identity. He has an MA (Honours) in History from the University of Glasgow, and has told stories in schools, libraries, festivals, sheltered housing and at private functions and gigs for many years. He is an experienced tour guide and storytelling is a central part of this work. As well as writing a weekly column called 'Tim's Tales' for the *East Lothian Courier*, he has also been involved in storytelling abroad as part of cultural programmes at universities in the Czech Republic and Portugal, and at schools and cultural events in Spain, Germany, Sweden and Slovakia. He lives in East Lothian.

www.facebook.com/Tim-Porteus-Storyteller

ABOUT THE ILLUSTRATOR

MAGS MACFARLANE was born and raised in East Lothian, and her deep knowledge of the landscape and traditions of the region has inspired her image-making since childhood. The drawings in this book reflect her passion for and connection with the area and its people. She is a graduate in Drawing and Painting from Edinburgh College of Art. A long career in art and design education gave her opportunities to work both within the classroom and in developing national learning materials for both teachers and students. She enjoys working in a variety of traditional materials, and in recent years has imaginatively embraced digital technology and the exciting multimedia possibilities it brings.

ACKNOWLEDGEMENTS

This book would have been impossible without the understanding and support of my wife, Katharina, to whom I give my heartfelt thanks. She has been a rock and support beyond the call of duty for any partner in a marriage. I am a very lucky man.

When Mags Nisbet-Macfarlane agreed to provide the illustrations for the stories, I quickly realised, as her beautiful drawings were revealed, that this was not going to be my book, but our book. A huge thanks to Mags for her dedication and passion in working with me on this, as her drawings have entwined with my words to greatly enhance the imagery of the stories.

So many people have provided kind words and support, and they include Donald Smith, Ros Parkyn, Alan and Claire Hunter, Gareth Jones, Lea Taylor, Carol Stobie, Brian and Caroline Tait, Ross Hamilton, Robert Scott and Suu Caledonia. There are many more who should be included and I thank them wholeheartedly.

In addition, I would like to thank my children, Mairi, Morvern, Manja, Skye and Lewis for constantly providing me with insights and motivation to explore stories. I want them to know just how important their contribution has been. Also my much loved departed mother, 'Granny Liz' to her grandchildren, who always gave support in her special way.

And finally, I would like to dedicate this book to the memory of Angie Townsend, who was an inspirational storyteller and singer. I owe her a huge debt, and more than one story in this collection has been influenced by her telling of the tale.

Angie is sadly missed by her family and friends, but the legacy of her storytelling, as well as her singing, is a cherished gift for us all.

FOREWORD

East Lothian is a unique part of Scotland. Due east and south-east of Edinburgh, it stretches between the Firth of Forth and the Lammermuir Hills, looking north to Fife and out to the open sea. There are harbours and islands, rich agricultural plains, steepled villages and ancient towns, and beyond, the further horizons of gently sloping hills. Between hill and sea, the people of East Lothian have laboured as fisher folk, agricultural workers, miners and craftsmen.

History has happened in East Lothian, as armies by sea and land have used this route in and out of Scotland. But there is also a rich local culture of myth, folk tale and song. This is a territory of Arthurian lore, of pioneering saints, vibrant old Scots, and early English influences. It is a layered, multi-storied region and in Tim Porteus, East Lothian has found its perfect storyteller.

Tim was brought up in Edinburgh's Old Town and on the East Lothian coast in the town of Prestonpans, to which he has returned to live with his family. He is a storyteller with endless curiosity and a bottomless capacity for engaging people of every age and culture. Naturally, Tim Porteus has become a touchstone of Lothian life, a regular columnist in the *East Lothian Courier*, and, as they say in Scotland, a 'kenspeckled figure'.

Yet, despite his fund of stories and writing, this is Tim Porteus's first published book. *East Lothian Folk Tales* is a delight and a must for all those living in or visiting East Lothian. Through these pages, landscape and community both come to life. But above all, it is Tim's humanity that shines through – his humour, compassion and endless curiosity. Tim has done his home turf proud with an excellent addition to the *Folk Tales* series. And along the way he demonstrates all the virtues of Scottish storytelling – entertainment, delight and profound attachment to your own place. All of these you are now invited to share in the traditional manner: 'yin day ... once upon a time ... wait till you hear this ...'

Please enjoy.

Donald Smith, 2017
Director, TRACS (Traditional Arts and Culture Scotland)

INTRODUCTION

A wee while back, I was shopping in a local supermarket in Prestonpans. As I waited in the queue, the sight of freshly cooked sausage rolls made me feel hungry. Of course, this is deliberate, for they place the hot food by the queue for the checkout, knowing that hungry customers will be tempted to ask for a snack.

'Anything else?' asked the assistant.

'Er, yes, a sausage roll please,' my mouth said.

And so I left the shop with the greasy sausage roll clasped in my guilty hands. The problem with sausage rolls is their flaky pastry disintegrates and makes a terrible mess when eaten. So I realised I must consume it before getting into the car. Anyway, I had bought it because I needed a quick snack, and so I turned the corner, faced a wall to ensure there were no witnesses, and began to heartily scoff.

I was halfway through when I heard a voice behind me.

'You're the storyteller aren't you?'

I turned round to see a young girl, perhaps around 14 or 15 years of age. Unfortunately, the half-consumed sausage roll meant I had bits of pastry all over me, and I felt very embarrassed!

'Em, aye, I am,' I said, trying to wipe away the mess from my mouth.

'I kent it,' she said, 'you telt me a story when I was in P2.'

I have told stories to local children many times and so couldn't remember her specifically, or the story. But she did. It had been over nine years since I'd told her the tale but she recounted it, and then told me how she'd told it at the time to her oldest sister, and that now her sister is a mother and that she has told it to her son.

'Just wanted tae, well, let ye ken, and say thanks,' she said.

At that moment her friends came out of the supermarket, looking for her. 'There you are, what you doing?' one asked.

'Oh nothing,' she said and suddenly walked away without acknowledging me or saying goodbye. I understood of course; talking to an old storyteller with sausage roll all over him isn't cool when you're a teenager.

It made my day, but this simple encounter revealed a deep truth about stories and storytelling: a story told to you can stay with you, and become an inheritance to pass on.

The stories in this book, I believe, are part of the inheritance of anyone who has an interest in East Lothian. They link to the county's landscape and the folk who have lived in and shaped it. They are a small selection of what is possible, but give a flavour of East Lothian life, its traditions and beliefs.

While there are some longer stories in this collection, I have written them all at a pace and length I hope will encourage readers to take them off the page and tell them. I personally never truly remember a story until I've told it. It's the engagement during the storytelling process, of eye to eye, mind to mind and heart to heart, which sparks the creative imagery which sears the tale in memory.

And so I have told these tales at events all over the county. Some are amusing, some eerie, some sad or tragic. History decorates some of them, yet the folk tradition speaks of the human condition, and for me some universal truths emerge in these stories.

East Lothian is such a fascinating and beautiful county, and I have tried to use stories that are located in different parts of it; from the wild heather-clad Lammermuirs, to the spectacular and varied coastline, and the lush farm and woodlands in between.

There are the voices of others in these tales, also. Angie Townsend was a fellow storyteller whose passion and skill in telling stories transfixed so many people, including myself. Her help with some of these tales cannot go unacknowledged, in particular the great legend of the birth of the Scottish flag.

My wife Katharina and my children have explored with me as I have sought to find the locations of the tales, and feel the atmosphere of the location. All my five children have in different ways become part of the stories, and I think that is as it should be, for we should all make stories part of who we are.

This book emerged from the stories I wrote for the *East Lothian Courier*, and the response from many of the readers of those tales. Often people would tell me what their favourite story was, usually one which resonated with them or kindled memory. In the writing of the tales I have sewn my own emotional connections to the characters and places which feature in them.

I cannot travel through the county without being conscious of the invisible tapestry of tales which covers it. When I walk in the footsteps of my early childhood by the shore of my home town, the pirate who founded it, and the legendary stone which is said to protect it, is never far from mind. The fairy stories and the magic creatures in the woods all jump at me when I travel into what, for me, is a land of mystery and wonder.

The looming volcanic hill of Traprain Law is a raised theatre for the performance of an ancient Celtic legend. And the corners of the county, with their ghosts, castles and strange goings on, echo the beliefs and lives of folk whose imagination we share when we enter the world of the stories they told. A field is never just a field once a story has seeped into its soil.

How much more interesting is a visit to the ancient Loth Stone, once you have heard the tale of King Loth's death, and the story of fairies dancing in its shadow? How much more can we get from a visit to the picturesque Canty Bay when we can see in our mind's eye the smuggled kegs that once littered its tidal foreshore? Can we ever visit North Berwick without a chuckling smile on our face once we have heard of the Gyre Carling's creation of it?

And who can sit in the woods by the kirk at Whittinghame, and not feel moved by the plight of the mother and her ghostly nameless son, or understand that a Tattie Bogle can be about more than scaring crows. Or journey up into the wilds of the Lammermuirs, and be chilled by the tales of past dark deeds committed in the mist? Who would not want to visit the lonely graves of Gilchriston once the love story had been told?

This collection of tales is necessarily limited, and so I am aware of how inadequate it is. It barely scratches the surface of what lies beneath East Lothian's landscape and experience. Yet I hope it can open the door to exploration, not just of the stories, but of the places that framed them. East Lothian remains a truly fascinating and beautiful place to live and visit, and never a day goes by that I don't appreciate the privilege of living here.

Tim Porteus

1

THE LEGEND OF THE SALTIRE

I understand that you good people of East Lothian have a particular reason to celebrate St Andrew's Day, but I thought I would take this opportunity to remind you that you do, in fact, also have your own saint, who actually lived and died in East Lothian. That saint is me, St Baldred. I know there are stories about me in this book, but I would like to take this opportunity to explain the background to the legend of the Saltire and my role in it.

The moment you drive into East Lothian, you are reminded of the fact that it is the birthplace of the Scottish flag. The legend has been told down the ages, of how St Andrew painted his cross in the sky and inspired the Scots and Picts to victory over Athelstan, King of the Angles.

I'm fine with all this of course, but I'm also going to be honest, St Columba would never say it out loud, but I know he was really hurt that he was overlooked for the role. He'd devoted the later part of his life to Scotland and died here. He travelled all over, getting blisters on his feet while converting people to Christianity. He even subdued the creature of Loch Ness, which is now a crucial part of the Scottish economy.

St Kentigern was a bit miffed too. As you know, his mother was from the area and he had been conceived in East Lothian, born in Fife and worked and buried in Glasgow. And I spent almost all my working life in East Lothian. I founded many churches here and there are holy wells with my name all over the county, which I personally blessed. But I do understand that I had mixed loyalties, so I wasn't expecting to receive a prayer. But poor St Columba, well, he was.

Don't get me wrong, we are all devoted to St Andrew and think he's done a great job, but the truth is he never set foot on Scottish soil. It was only a tooth, an arm bone, a kneecap and a finger that were brought to Scotland by a monk called St Rule. I know these relics were kept at a place which became known as St Andrews, but the man himself never came here, did he? He did all his work in Greece and the area about.

The truth is, he actually doesn't know that much about Scotland, except what we have told him. However, having said that, I do understand that St Andrew was one of the Apostles, and St Columba could never claim that.

But I'd like to let you into what happened that day. You see, St Andrew didn't actually see most of it, he was so busy. He asked us to keep an eye on the situation, as I knew the area and St Columba was so concerned. So in a sense we were coordinating things and saw it first-hand. Here is what happened.

The whole thing began with a cattle raid by the Scots and Picts in AD 832. You see, at this time East Lothian wasn't part of early Scotland, it was in fact part of Northumbria, as it had been when I lived there (hence my mixed loyalties). But to the north of the Forth it was the land of the Picts. Their king was Angus (Oengus) who ruled most of the north-east of what is now Scotland, from Fife to the Orkneys.

It was Angus who came up with the plan for a great cattle raid. At the time, I thought it was a bad idea, but of course he didn't listen. He managed to get the support of Eochaidh, who was king of the Scots of Dalriada in the west.

I have to say, it was interesting to see Picts and Scots come together like this. I think it was because the Northumbrians were seen as a common enemy, and this show of military strength and unity would make the Northumbrians think twice before advancing northwards.

The cattle raid was a great success, but that was part of the trouble. I looked down on all this and could see that the Northumbrian leader Athelstan was raging. It was obvious he was going to try and punish the invading Celts!

There were so many cattle it took ages to herd them back into safe territory, and so Angus found himself way behind schedule. It was nail-biting to watch as the Northumbrians caught up with his force at the mouth of the River Tyne.

I could see Angus was concerned, he hadn't planned this. But now he had no time to run, so he started looking for a good defensive position. He found it in the Peffer Valley, near a place called Markle, close to East Linton. Here the river would be an obstacle for Athelstan's forces, and the open space provided good ground for an attack. The surrounding raised ground also meant lookouts could be posted.

I remember St Columba being very concerned that the odds looked very bad, the Northumbrians had a force four times larger than Angus's and Eochaidh's combined force. Angus knew this from his scouts, and so he led his men in prayer.

This was the awkward moment. The saint they called on was not St Columba, who was watching and waiting for the call, but St Andrew. Angus promised to make him the patron saint if he would come to his aid. St Columba took it well, but I could tell he was deeply disappointed not to be given this opportunity.

The irony was when St Andrew got the message, he was so busy he delegated the task of watching over the Scots and Picts to St Columba anyway, and asked me to help out because of my local connections. He gave us instructions to inform him when action was needed. Of course, we gladly accepted this task.

That night, before the battle, we could feel the tension amongst the Scots and Picts. Angus and his men tried to get some sleep under the stars, but it was not easy. Everyone knew that in the morning Athelstan's mighty force would arrive.

St Andrew asked us how it was going, and we explained the situation. 'Hmm, what do you suggest?' he asked.

'Well, I think the Scots need something to boost their confidence,' suggested St Columba, 'perhaps you could assure Angus of your support since he prayed to you?' St Andrew nodded and so that's what he did.

He appeared to Angus in a dream, saying, 'Fear not, you will have victory tomorrow be assured, and a heavenly sign will show the truth of this.'

St Andrew then left. I just assumed he'd arranged the heavenly sign, but I think it slipped his mind as he was so busy.

The morning arrived with the sound of thousands of men approaching. But thanks to his reassuring dream, Angus was now sure of victory. He cheered his men with the story of his night-time visit from St Andrew and they were uplifted by it.

I could hardly look as the battle raged, it was so bloody and brutal. At one point the Northumbrians tried to cross the Peffer at the ford by Prora, but they were blocked by barricades of hastily cut down hawthorn.

But eventually Athelstan's main force encircled Angus and his men, and it seemed all would be lost as the Northumbrians had

such overwhelming numbers. It was brutal, no wonder the field there became known as the bloody lands. St Columba went over to St Andrew and said to him, politely, 'Ahem, I think that now would be a good moment for that heavenly sign you promised, St Andrew.'

'Oh yes, of course, thank you for reminding me,' said St Andrew. So he came over, had a quick think, then cleared the clouds and made his sign: a white inverted cross against a deep blue sky! I must admit, it was an impressive sight.

Well, when the Picts and Scots saw this they cheered, and their bodies were charged with a new spirit of confidence and belief. Their renewed fighting spirit sent the Northumbrians reeling and the tide of battle turned!

Athelstan himself refused to give up, and his head was sliced off by a Celtic sword at a place thereafter known as Athelstaneford. The head was kept as a trophy and later displayed on a pole in Fife! I didn't approve of that of course, awful.

And so that's how it happened. It's great that St Andrew's cross is the Scottish flag, and he is the patron saint. I'm not jealous or anything, we're saints, we don't do jealousy. I'm very happy my old stomping ground is now part of Scotland, and St Columba says he's fine with it all. After all, he still has the Loch Ness legend to his name.

Now I know there is a big question mark over whether all this happened, because there is no written historical evidence for it, and some people have suggested my memory is faulty and influenced by the constant hearing of the story. I can't comment on that. I do accept that there are other stories as to how Athelstaneford got its name, but just remember: a lot of things weren't written down, but they still happened! And likewise, a lot of things were written down that didn't happen! That's the thing about legends, I suppose.

I just thought I'd take the opportunity to put a new perspective on one of East Lothian's greatest legends, and remind people that there are places to visit associated with me too.

I hope you enjoy the book.

St Baldred.

2

St Baldred's Boat

The Bass Rock looms out of the sea close to North Berwick, its cliffs turned white in the spring because of the thousands of nesting seabirds. It is an impressive, almost surreal sight, and legend tells us it was on this rocky island that St Baldred spent much of his time in prayer and quiet contemplation.

To leave the island he would take the short route by boat to Seacliff, where a cave and ancient dwelling still bear his name. Although it was usually a short journey, it could be perilous, especially in bad weather or fading light. There was a shelf of rock which lay below the surface at high tide, but was exposed at low tide. It lay between the Bass Rock and the shoreline; right in the middle of the route taken by local fishermen. Many boats had their hulls ripped by it at high tide, and at low tide strong winds could blow boats onto its jagged edge, wrecking them completely.

After witnessing a near fatal incident on this rock, St Baldred decided that he must try to do something about this danger to the lives of his flock. He prayed for guidance and soon afterwards he came ashore and spoke to the local fishermen.

'I want you to take me to the rock at low tide,' he said to them, 'then leave me there.'

The fishermen were horrified. They had no idea why the holy man wanted to do this, but they knew how dangerous it would be; 'when the tide rises you will be swept by the waves into the sea, please do not ask us to do this,' they pleaded.

But St Baldred was insistent. 'Have faith,' he scolded them. 'I know what I am doing. I have prayed and God has answered me.'

At low tide they reluctantly rowed him to the rock. The sea swirled and crashed against the edge and it was not easy to find a place to drop the saint off. More than once they tried to persuade the holy man to abandon the idea. But he was determined.

Eventually St Baldred managed to scramble onto the rock and the fishermen rowed away, leaving him there alone, as he'd asked. But they knew that the tide would soon rise, so they stayed nearby, ready to rescue him. But when St Baldred saw this he repeated his call to 'Have faith!'. They rowed a little further away, but not too far, so they could still watch from a distance.

St Baldred stood on the rock's highest point and raised his arms to the sky calling out to God. The fishermen watched with disbelieving eyes as the great rock slowly rose up, and seemed to float like a boat. Then, with the holy man balancing on it like a surfer on a giant surf board, the rock began to move towards the mainland.

St Baldred carefully navigated the rock towards the sandy beach at Seacliff. Then he lowered his arms and the rock slowed down and came to rest. It settled into the sand, and St Baldred was able to walk off it onto the beach. The holy man turned and smiled at a job well done, and fell to his knees to give thanks for the miracle.

Now the rock was in a safer position, close to the shore. It opened a rock-free channel between the Bass and the mainland. Local people flocked to him to give thanks. But the holy man told them, 'Do not thank me, give thanks to the Lord your God, and have faith in Him'. They bowed their heads and nodded in reverence. St Baldred had shown the power of faith in God!

So much time has passed since these days, but the rock remains where St Baldred anchored it. It's called St Baldred's Boat and can be seen clearly from Seacliff Beach, and reached from there at low tide. These days a prominent beacon with a cross decorates the spot where the holy man navigated his 'boat'.

There are many places associated with St Baldred in East Lothian, including his holy wells. But it is perhaps his 'boat', and the story of how he navigated it, which leaves the greatest impression on the imagination.

3

St Baldred's Last Miracle

St Baldred spent a lot of time on the Bass Rock in a small chapel he built. In truth, it wasn't really a chapel, just a simple cell. It was a place where St Baldred went to rest and pray and be close to God. It was hard work being a missionary, and having me and God time was vital. The swelling sea and the birds gave constant noise, but it was the sound of creation, and he loved it.

On his last visit to the Bass Rock he felt very weary. His bones ached, and he felt his soul being called. Sure enough, soon afterwards he departed to meet his Lord and Saviour, his earthly work done. Or so he thought.

The discovery of his body was first greeted with wailing and grief, but this soon gave way to a great argument. His followers were from different communities in what is now East Lothian. While he was alive he could serve them all equally, but now only one place could be chosen to lay his body to rest.

The people of Auldhame, Tyninghame and Prestonkirk, who had all been united by the word of God, were now in conflict over the issue of where to bury the holy man they all had loved and been devoted to equally. St Baldred must have been saddened to see his flock so readily forget his teachings and fight over his physical body.

But who now could mediate between these communities, united in grief but separated over the issue of where the holy man should rest? Fortunately there was good guidance at hand. A wise man within the church, who had known St Baldred well when he lived, soothed the tempers of his followers.

'You must pray all night,' he told them, 'and in the morning an answer will be forthcoming.' And so they all followed his advice. Representatives of all three communities spent the night in vigil and prayer in the chapel where Baldred's body lay.

And in the morning, just before sunrise, the wise man visited them. He first asked the people of Auldhame, 'Have your prayers been answered?'

'We prayed all night,' they said, 'and in the morning we heard God's answer within our souls.'

'And what was this answer?' asked the wise man.

'God wishes the burial to be at Auldhame, where his holy remains will lie in view of the sea and his island sanctuary,' they replied.

Then the wise man turned to the people of Tyninghame. They too had prayed all night and had received an answer from God.

'And what was God's answer to you?' asked the wise man.

'God wishes the burial to be at Tyninghame,' they replied, 'so he lies close to the river in whose water he used to baptise so many.'

And finally, the wise man asked the congregation at Prestonkirk. They likewise had prayed all night and been give an answer.

'The Lord wishes the burial to be at Prestonkirk, so he lies close to his sacred healing well,' they replied.

'So the Lord has spoken and given you his answer,' said the wise man.

There were murmurings amongst the assembled. 'But who has the right answer?' asked one. 'How can God give us three different answers?' demanded another. 'They must be lying,' said another. Discord and conflict were about to break out once again.

The wise man raised his arms and calmed everyone. 'We are all united in grief for the loss of our holy brother, but let us celebrate that he now sits with the Lord.'

The sunrise suddenly beamed light through the small window of the chapel, revealing the place where Baldred's body had been lain. But now there lay not one, but three bodies, all wrapped up ready for burial. All three were St Baldred, identical in every respect. There were gasps from the people, who then fell to their knees in prayer and thanksgiving for the miracle.

'The Lord has answered your prayers, now in unity go and bury our beloved holy brother,' said the wise man.

And so St Baldred was buried in all three parishes, which is why today each one can equally claim to be the resting place of the saint.

It was St Baldred's last legendary miracle, and an ingenious way to avoid conflict and division amongst his followers after he had departed his earthly life.

4

THE HOLY PRINCESS OF EAST LOTHIAN

There can hardly be a more iconic image of East Lothian than Traprain Law. This great volcanic hill dominates the surrounding countryside, and despite a slice being removed by twentieth-century mining operations, it has lost none of its power to impress.

On its broad summit was once a great fortress, known as Dunpelder or Dunpender, home to the great Celtic tribe called the Gododdin (known to the Romans as the Votadini). The head of this tribe was called King Loth (or Lot). Such was his power and prestige that the name Lothian is said to be derived from his name. He was the brother-in-law of the legendary King Arthur.

And so in choosing a husband for his daughter, Thenew, he decided upon what he considered a suitable match.

'You shall marry Prince Owain,' commanded Loth, for he was a prince from the Celtic kingdom of Rheged, a suitable match that would also enhance Loth's position.

But Thenew felt no affection for the prince. 'Father, I beg you, I do not wish to marry him,' pleaded Thenew.

Soon her pleadings grew into defiance. Her refusal to obey his will enraged King Loth. If he could not control his own daughter, how could he be respected as a king and leader of men! He must teach her a lesson, one in which she would be glad to marry a man of status like Owain.

And so he banished her from her fortress home and forced her to live with a family of swineherds, by the Lammermuir Hills. She would live amongst the muck and dirt of a lowly family, far from the reverence of her royal position. This humiliation would teach her the meaning of life! Soon she would be begging to be freed from such a lowly existence, and agree to marry Owain.

But in that muck and dirt amongst the swine she found a new peace within her heart. She had become a Christian, and to live the simple life of a poor peasant was no hardship for her. What is more, she was in love with the son of the family who looked after her. He loved her dearly in return and when her father's spies watched her she could not hide her happiness. She felt not poor, but richer than she had ever been.

The king's plan was not working! He smashed his hand on the table when given the news of his daughter's joy. And Owain's anger at being rejected fed dark thoughts. 'Take her anyway,' he was advised, 'and once you have taken her she will be yours regardless of her will.'

Her happiness and contented spirit were too much to bear for the men who wanted to control her. So Owain resolved to take her by force. Like a fox he crept in the darkness close to the swineherd's home, in disguise as a woman. He waited for the moment Thenew was alone. Then he raped her. But his violence didn't break her for she still refused to submit to his will.

'You still choose to live amongst the swine?' Owain sneered.

'Even the swine are better than you can ever be,' replied Thenew defiantly.

But soon after, her belly began to swell and the king's spies reported that she was with child. This was a dishonour that King Loth could not tolerate. He brought Thenew back to his fortress. He would listen to nothing she said. Her dishonourable state was plain for all to see.

He sentenced her to death by stoning! Yet no one wanted to be held directly responsible for the death of this young princess, no one wanted to cast the first stone. But the sentence must be carried out, the king's honour and authority were at stake.

And so the stone that would kill her would be the cliff that plunged from the fortress. She was placed upon a cart, which was then taken to the edge. She closed her eyes and prayed, for forgiveness for herself, but also for her father and those who had done her wrong.

The cart was then pushed over the cliff edge by a group of chosen warriors. This way, no one man could be said to have caused her death. Tears were shed by many at the sight, and few could bear to watch.

As the cart plunged down the cliff it was smashed and broken on the rocks, finally coming to a crashing halt over 300 feet below. A group of Thenew's friends waiting at the base of the cliff clenched their chests with horror at the sight of the now crumpled and destroyed chariot, under which lay Thenew. They knew her body must be broken and bloodied, and nobody could have survived such a dreadful crash. They just hoped that her end had been quick.

But then, unbelievably, Thenew emerged. Both she and her unborn child were alive! Her friends fell to their knees and gave thanks to God. They helped Thenew from the wreckage and she prayed with them.

The pole from the cart splintered away and buried itself into the ground like a giant spear. From where it pierced the ground, a spring gushed forth. A holy well was now at the base of the rock.

'What dark magic is this?' cried her father's advisors. 'It is witchcraft,' said the king. 'No sire, a miracle from God!' proclaimed her friends. 'Very well,' said the king to his daughter, 'if this be your God and he wishes to let you and your child live, then I will set you adrift on the sea, and let your God save you.'

And so she was taken to Aberlady Bay, then known as 'the river mouth of the stench' because of the fish thrown from the fishermen's boats. From here she was placed in a coracle, a small round canoe, made of hide. She shuddered with fear as her small craft was pulled from the shore and taken out to sea, then set adrift on the outgoing tide.

The tiny vessel drifted towards the open sea, the water lapping at Thenew's feet as she desperately tried to avoid capsizing. She frantically scooped the water with her hands, but the land began to vanish and the water grew darker, and the coracle began to sink.

She approached the Isle of May, but she drifted helplessly past it. Then she reached a small rock some distance from the island. It was slippery and covered with seaweed, but she clung onto it, her fingers desperately trying to find a hold.

But her body was soaked and numb with the cold, and her hands frozen. The waves crashed over her, and she slipped from the rock back into the swirling sea. Strands of her hair remained entangled in the seaweed, so the rock thereafter became known as Maiden Hair Rock.

The sea was claiming her and her unborn child and so in desperation she prayed to God. The fish which had followed her from Aberlady Bay now began to swim around her, then seals appeared and gulls circled above. She was no longer alone. She scrambled back into her small half-sunk vessel, and now it began

to move back into the Firth. Night began to fall and exhaustion overcame her. She closed her eyes, and slipped into unconsciousness.

When the morning mist cleared, a shore appeared before her. There she landed, by Culross in Fife. It was just as well, for there she gave birth to her son, whom she called Kentigern, meaning 'first lord' in her Celtic language.

At that moment some shepherds found her, took pity and warmed her by a fire. They were good men and took news of the maiden with a newly born boy to the local holy man.

He was St Serf who helped raise the child, who became one of the most important saints in Scotland, often called St Mungo, meaning 'my dear friend', patron saint of Glasgow. And so began another great story!

But what of King Loth? His vengeance was now directed towards the swineherd, for he had assumed the poor boy who loved Thenew was to blame for her dishonour. He tried to hunt him down, but the young lad retreated into marshy ground.

And then the hunter became the hunted. The young lad lay in wait for the king close to his fortress home. As Loth passed by, the swineherd threw a spear which pierced and killed him. The legendary King Loth now lay dead in the shadow of his fortress, killed by the man who truly loved his daughter. Tradition says he was buried where he had fallen, and a great stone was erected on the spot as a memorial, forever after known as the Loth Stane.

It is still to be seen, and although its location has been moved slightly, it stands as a memorial to one of East Lothian's great legends.

5

THE WIZARD OF YESTER

In the year 1263, the Viking longships were a constant threat in the seas around Scotland. The King of Scotland was Alexander III. He was a young man and his attempts to challenge Viking control of the Western Isles had stirred the wrath of the Norwegian King Haakon, who was now assembling a great invasion fleet.

The young Scottish king needed advice and support from those he trusted, and there was one man in the realm who he believed could help him. This man was Sir Hugh Giffard, known to history as the Wizard of Yester. He was renowned for his magical powers, and it was said these included the ability to see into the future!

And so the king set off for Yester Castle to consult this great and unusual nobleman. When Alexander arrived at this grand castle, it seemed Sir Hugh was not at home. There were no doorbells in those days, so the king blew his horn. The sound reverberated around the castle, bouncing off the great walls.

After a few moments, Sir Hugh appeared from a small entrance by the wall.

'Your Majesty,' he said with a bow.

The king studied Sir Hugh's attire. He had a cloak of fox skins, wore a pointed hat and shoes marked with a cross and other strange markings. Around his neck hung a pentacle decorated with stars. And Sir Hugh stood before the king holding a sword.

'Your Majesty, I was deep below in my chamber when I heard the blast of your horn. I had no time to change my attire.'

'That I see,' replied the king.

The wizard smiled and nodded. 'But I know why you have come to see me,' he said. 'You seek advice and hope that my powers can show you what the future holds. I am afraid I cannot tell you this.'

Alexander protested, 'But you are a man of great magic, surely you know a way to help your king to see what is to come in these days of such peril, so I may rule this realm with wisdom?'

Sir Hugh hesitated for a moment, then spoke softly, as if someone may be listening.

'Your Majesty, there is a way. But the danger is great.'

'Tell me more,' said the king.

'There are elfins who can foretell what is to come. I once summoned one to my chamber. The spell I cast was the strength of oak, but the elfin stubbornly refused to tell. Only when faced with a greater force than he will he reveal what he knows.'

'I am the king,' replied Alexander, 'he will fear me.'

Sir Hugh nodded. 'Indeed, you are the king, backed by God's grace, but there is danger in this quest, Your Majesty. If the elfin does not fear you, then I cannot guarantee your life.'

'Place him in front of me and by God, I swear when he sees my royal sword he will talk!'

'Bravely spoken, Your Majesty, you are a worthy king with the blood of the great Malcolm in your veins,' replied the wizard. His face then took on a serious shade.

'The elfin lives just over there,' he said, pointing to a hill close to the castle. 'At midnight, you must go alone with your steed and seek the entrance by the ancient ramparts. Stand by the threshold but do not enter. Blow your horn and the elfin will come to you. He will appear, not as himself, but in the guise of your worst enemy. Do not delay, Your Majesty, with royal courage charge him with your lance. If he fears you he will tell you what he knows.'

'And if he fears me not?' asked the king.

'Then, Your Majesty, your life will be in peril,' replied Sir Hugh.

The king was young and brave, and this warning did not deter him. So as midnight approached he rode to the hill. It was deathly cold with a sliver of moon. He found the entrance, but

as instructed did not enter. He put his horn to his lips, and blew. The trumpet sound filled the stillness of the night. Then the king heard rumbling and groaning from below ground. Something had awoken!

A figure emerged, sitting proudly on a demon horse. The king knew the elfin would be in the form of Scotland's worst enemy. But Alexander was taken aback. This elfin knight had not appeared in the shape of King Haakon! It was of Edward, the King of England!

'But how could this be?' thought Alexander. 'It is Haakon's ships that threaten my shore, and good Edward is far away in holy war. I must know what this means.'

And so with great courage the king lowered his lance and charged the elfin knight. What an eerie combat, under the midnight moon! But the king's courage was matched with jousting skill. He unhorsed the elfin, who fell to the ground. The king quickly dismounted and drew his sword.

'Now, demon, you will tell me all you know of what is to come,' said Alexander.

And so the elfin spoke. He told the king of how Haakon's men would fall at Largs, and Haakon himself never return to his home. But fire and blood were not far away, coming not from the north, but the south, with Edward leading the rage!

As Walter Scott said: 'long afterwards did Scotland know, fell Edward was her deadliest foe!'

The king returned from this night with great confidence. But he was not without injury. A splinter of the elfin's lace had grazed his cheek. It was an insignificant cut, so at first he thought nothing of it. But it would not truly heal, and every year, on the anniversary of that eerie night combat, the wound would open and bleed.

When the king told Sir Hugh of this strange wound, he nodded knowingly and said, 'Bold as you were that night, Your Majesty, you still pay the penance.'

But Alexander now secretly knew of the danger that Scotland faced from Edward I of England. But Alexander could do nothing to defend his realm from this threat because he died in a tragic accident before the invasion from the south. In fact, his death precipitated the events which led to this war with England.

The wizard's old castle was destroyed during this war. Its ruins now hide in the woods near the town of Gifford. But search carefully and you will find the infamous chamber called 'Goblin Ha' below the ruins. It is entered by a small side door, and legend tells us this underground chamber was made by goblins for Sir Hugh. He used his magic to harness their skills, and it was in this vaulted chamber that he performed much of his magic.

It still has an eerie and powerful atmosphere. A staircase from the chamber leads you further down into the darkness, possibly to a well. It's now blocked, as locals had tales that it actually led to hell itself!

Take care if you visit this mysterious place, for as Walter Scott said, some believe the elfin warrior still waits for those who dare to challenge him:

> Yet still the nightly spear and shield
> The Elfin Warrior doth wield,
> Upon the brown hill's breast;
> And many a knight hath proved his chance,
> In the charmed ring to break a lance ...

6

THE MAGIC PEAR

The daughter of the Wizard of Yester was getting married. The wizard was otherwise known as Hugh Gifford, a nobleman of great repute in East Lothian. On this day his daughter Margaret (or Marion in some accounts) was marrying into another East Lothian noble family, the Brouns of Colstoun.

It was a fine autumn day and the bridal party arrived at the church with Hugh ready to give his daughter away. As they walked towards the church, Hugh suddenly peeled away from his daughter and walked towards a pear tree. He studied it for a moment, then with great care picked a pear from the tree.

'Father, what are you doing? I am to be wed today. Will you not walk with me?' asked his confused daughter.

Hugh stood for a moment and cast his hand over the pear. The bridal group stood in silence, wondering what the father of the bride was up to.

Hugh then returned to his daughter.

'Here,' he said, 'this is my gift for you, my daughter, and for your husband to be.'

'That is not much of a dowry, sire!' joked one of the noble guests.

'Keep it safe,' said Hugh to his daughter, 'for this pear, if lovingly kept, will ensure prosperity in your life and of those that follow. Although ripe and full of sweetness, eat it not, as it must be preserved with great care.'

In normal circumstances, a father giving a pear to his daughter as a wedding present would have caused some ridicule, but Hugh Gifford was of course no ordinary man. He was known as

the Wizard of Yester for good reason, as legend tells us he was a conjurer of magic and spells.

And so his Marion not only accepted the gift, she kept it safe and untouched in a silver casket, away from sunlight and bad air. It was guarded as an ancient family treasure and for many generations the family prospered, just as the wizard had predicted.

Then, over 400 years later, George of Colstoun married Lady Elizabeth Mackenzie. She was introduced to the legend of the pear, and when told the story was understandably keen to see it. Surely after so many years there would be nothing left of it, she thought.

But when the casket was opened, she was astonished to see that the pear looked as delicious and ripe as the day Hugh had picked it! The temptation and curiosity were too much, and before anyone could stop her, she took a bite! 'Nooo!' called out her husband as she did so, but too late. The pear had a bitemark on it.

Her husband was very upset, holding his head in his hands.

'Och, it's only a pear,' said Elizabeth defensively, but then seeing the reaction of her husband she began to wonder if perhaps it was a serious mistake. 'Do you really think the legend is true?' she asked. Soon she would discover the consequences of her bite.

Not long afterwards, her husband had to sell the estate to his brother Robert, due to gambling debts. This was unfortunate, but at least the estate was kept in the family.

But more misfortune followed.

In May 1703, Robert was returning to Colstoun from Edinburgh. It had been raining heavily and there had also been some thawing of snow on the upper hills. The land was awash with water and the Colstoun Water had turned into a torrent. Robert was in a coach with his four children and his wife.

The coach driver had a difficult job. The course of the ford across the water was not clearly visible, as white bubbling torrents were streaming over it. But he knew that Robert and his family were keen to be home and so he compelled the horses forward.

He misjudged the way. The coach veered onto its side, throwing all the occupants into the raging water. Robert's wife and their two daughters wore supported crinoline dresses which fluffed up, creating something akin to lily-shaped boats around them, floating them eventually to the safety of the riverbank. It must have been an unusual, even comical sight! But their dresses saved their lives.

Robert and his two sons were not so lucky. They were swept away by the angry water and drowned.

Such misfortune in such a short time. Was this a curse because the pear had been damaged? The family's fortunes did slowly improve thereafter, but keeping the pear safe from any further damage became very important.

And so the Pear of Colstoun has been kept safe ever since at Colstoun House. It even survived a fire in 1907. It is kept in a silver box, with the teeth marks of Lady Elizabeth still visible.

It is described as a 'cherished symbol and insignia of the Brouns of Colstoun'.

7

THE GYRE CARLING

There are many stories of the Gyre Carling, but it has been told that she was in fact a horrible-looking hag who lived in a grim chamber, some say not far from Gullane. She was an ogress with a cruel and unpleasant character, and she was to be avoided at all costs.

Her favourite food was the flesh of Christian men. She'd capture them, sook their brains out and then lick out their innards for pudding. With such a diet, we may not be surprised to discover that she had a terrible flatulence problem. When wind passed from between her gruesome buttocks, sea birds could fall down dead from the stench, and saplings uproot from the force of it.

Now, you might think that nobody could possibly fall in love with such a hideous creature. Yet, as they say, love is blind. There was a shepherd called Blasour who was smitten when he saw her. Well, in truth it was a certain part of her he loved. He was utterly transfixed by her lips, her powerful red gaping lips! He had never been baptised and so he believed he would not be on her menu. He had sleepless nights thinking of her lips, and wished he could find a way to woo the ogress, so he could kiss them!

Yet his attempts to woo her failed miserably. He sent her flowers, sang her songs and recited romantic verse, but none of this worked. She was rude and unpleasant to him and told him to go away. Yet this didn't put him off, and he spent long evenings weeping and wailing because he desired her so much. Eventually he came up with an idea he thought could work!

He set about capturing moles, hundreds of them. It was no easy task, but the path of true love is often just hard work! His plan was

simple: he would set this army of moles free by her chamber, and their digging, he hoped, would cause it to collapse. She would then be homeless, and he would offer her shelter in his home. Perhaps in time she would learn to love him or, at the very least, allow him to kiss those lips!

And so he crept one evening to the edge of her chamber, and let loose a multitude of the wee animals, who immediately set about digging and undermining its foundations. But the ogress acted quickly, taking her great club and bashing the poor creatures the moment they popped their heads into her chamber. By morning the moles were dead or had fled.

But the ogress was baffled as to how this infestation had happened. Then she saw the sack, and realised it was that annoying shepherd who had tried to win her over with flowers and songs. How dare he try and make her homeless in order to force her to be with him!

And so, after asking a crow where he lived, she crept up into the Lammermuir Hills one evening. When she reached his house, he was sleeping. A noise made him open his eyes, and above him he saw the ogress. She had ripped his roof off and was now leaning over him.

The sight of those ruby red lips smiling down at him lifted his heart! His plan, he thought, had worked quicker than even he had hoped. But the smile turned into a wicked grin as the ogress lifted her huge arms. Her club was clasped in her hairy hands, and she brought it down onto the shepherd's chest and stomach with all the force she could muster.

The blow was deadly, and split him open. As he writhed in agony his intestines oozed out. It was a sight of horror, but the ogress thought his seeping insides looked like porridge. She found this hilarious and started to laugh. She laughed and laughed, smacking her sides, unable to stop, so funny she thought this sight was.

Well, when people have a flatulence problem and laugh uncontrollably they can, shall we say, lose control. And this was the case with the Gyre Carling, for as she laughed hysterically she let out an enormous fart, so loud it woke people in nearby villages. Indeed, such had been the force of her laughter, the ogress had passed more than just wind, and it flew over the county and landed by the sea with a great thud and dollop!

And so in the morning, people who lived in the area now called North Berwick could hardly believe their eyes. For just inland, there was a huge mound which hadn't been there before. And it is still there of course, but thankfully now solid and dry.

It's called North Berwick Law. Geologists will tell you something about volcanic remains, but according to this old tale, this major East Lothian landmark was created by a flatulent ogress!

8

THE FAIRY
TOURNAMENT

There is an old standing stone in the shadow of Traprain Law which, according to legend, is the burial place of King Loth, who once ruled the Goddodin Celtic tribe. His stronghold on Traprain Law was once a great hill fort.

Yet this stone has another tale attached to it. For it was here the wee folk of East Lothian have their great fairy tournaments. They are played out at night in secret, under a magical sparkling diamond which is placed atop the stone. We know this because they were once seen by a local man called Tam.

One evening, around 200 years ago, Tam was walking home along the road south of Traprain Law. The moonshine gave him just enough light to see his way, and the ancient hill was a silhouetted background.

Then he saw a strange brightness beaming from the fields further ahead. Tam wasn't aware of a house being there, and anyway, it was a light even brighter than a hundred candles could make. Perhaps it was a fire he thought. But flames flicker, and this was an intense light flooding the area. Tam was understandably curious.

If truth be told, he was more than merry, and this gave him the courage to investigate the strange light. He crept as quietly as he could towards its origin and as he got closer he could hear laughter, singing and music.

It sounded like a party or ceilidh, yet there was something eerie and unusual in the manner of the voices. Tam's instinct told him to be very careful, so he lay down and moved like a lizard towards the gathering. He peered through a small gap in the hedge and his jaw dropped at the sight his disbelieving eyes saw.

Fairies were dancing around the Loth Stane, to music that was so beguiling that Tam found himself resisting the desire to join in. Yet he was not too drunk to remember that fairies have a great dislike of being spied upon, and that their music can enchant a passer-by and entice him into their realm from which he may never return.

He was in danger, but this mesmerising spectacle was just too wonderful to peel away from. Some of the wee folk were playing musical instruments while others danced reels and jigs. There was food he didn't readily recognise and the whole scene was floodlit by what looked like a diamond on top of the standing stone. Wisps of sparkles floated from the diamond, like bright tiny stars floating in the evening air.

Then Tam came to his senses. He must leave now, lest he be discovered, or tempted to join in. But he knew he couldn't keep his discovery a secret. He must tell his family, and show them. They would be safer in numbers from any fairy enchantment he reckoned.

As quietly as he could, Tam slid backwards, and when far enough away to be out of earshot, he stood up and ran with all his might back home to tell what he'd seen.

He burst into his home, hardly able to speak from the running.

'Ye maun come tae see this!' he yelled out to his startled wife and family.

'Yer fou agin, Tam,' his wife said.

'Naw naw hen, aye weel, mebbe a wee bit, but ye maun come an see whit I've seen,' replied Tam, still half breathless.

'And …' his wife said, standing with arms folded and waiting unconvinced for whatever he had to say.

'There were wee folk, hunners o' them, haein a tournament. The great Loth Stane stood in the midst o' this spectacle, as if watching. Even though it wis nicht, they danced and played their games in the licht which came frae a great diamond, which wis atop the stane. It caught the moon's licht then sparkled it ower the assembled host o' wee folk sae it wis as bricht as daylicht!'

We can imagine it took some time for him to persuade his family he was not totally drunk, but his excitement and determination to show them paid off. They eventually agreed to venture into the night with him to see this amazing spectacle. Some of his neighbours, curious to see what the commotion had been about, came too.

Sure enough, as they approached the foothill of Traprain Law they saw an eerie brightness.

'Telt ye,' said Tam. The light was emanating from the area around the Loth Stane and was shimmering into the sky. They approached as quietly as they could. Soon the sound of laughter, talking and singing could be heard. Then there was music.

Tam led the way, walking as carefully as he could. But more feet make more noise. His neighbours were too keen to witness for themselves the unbelievable sight of a fairy tournament, and in their haste to get there, they walked carelessly. Someone stepped on a twig, which snapped.

In an instant it was dark. But the wee folk were still there, listening in the still of the night for another noise. Tam put his finger to his mouth to tell the others to be absolutely still and quiet.

But an unbearable desire to sneeze formed in the nose of Tam's wife. She held it with her hands, squeezed her nose tight with thumb and forefinger. Her eyes bulged and ears popped as she desperately tried to subdue the sneeze. But it was determined to surface and she just couldn't hold it in any longer. When it escaped it was half sneeze, half barking sound.

That was it. In the darkness the sound of hundreds of scuffling little feet could be heard as the wee folk fled back into fairy land.

In the morning, when Tam and the others returned to investigate in daylight, there was no sign of the wee folk, or indeed the diamond that had given them light.

But there were small footprints all over the ground, which proved to Tam he hadn't imagined it all.

THOMAS THE RHYMER MAKES HIS MARK IN DUNBAR

Thomas the Rhymer is a well-known character in Scottish folklore. He was a real person, and came from Ercildoune in the Borders, a place now called Earlston. The remains of his tower house can still be seen there, although most people who drive past it on the A68 never notice the partly hidden ruins of Thomas's former home.

His encounter with the queen of the fairies as he rested under a tree at Huntly Bank, close to the River Tweed, is one of Scotland's famous legendary tales. The kiss of this beautiful queen of the otherworld took him away for seven years into the realm of fairies and elves.

He must have been a man of some character, as the queen seems to have fallen in love with him and released him back into our world with some reluctance. Her gift of an apple gave Thomas the power to see into the future, but also an inability to tell a lie. This transformed Thomas into a legendary seer.

And so Thomas of Ercildoune became known as Thomas the Rhymer. He was a harpist, poet, balladeer and storyteller. When we combine this with a claim that he could foretell the future, we can understand why he was a popular guest or entertainer. He was even, so it seems, a bard at the court of King Alexander III.

So why does he make an appearance in a collection of folk tales from East Lothian? Well, the answer is that he made his mark in Dunbar.

Thomas's feudal overlord was Patrick, the Earl of March and Dunbar, and in early spring 1286 the earl summoned Thomas to his great castle on the shores of the Firth of Forth. The scene was set for the prophesy that would confirm Thomas's reputation as a genuine seer, and it was in the great castle of Dunbar that this happened.

It would be true to say that the arrival of Thomas at the castle created a mixture of anticipation and cynicism. Thomas must have known he had been called upon to perform and impress. But he was not intimidated, after all, he had performed in the court of the king.

It was a day of high winds and angry seas, the waves crashing against the rocks giving Dunbar Castle an atmospheric background. It was not an intimate family occasion that Thomas had been invited to. The earl had asked many visitors to his castle for this event, and many looked forward to meeting a man of growing reputation.

Thomas told tales and sang songs, entertaining his noble audience well. He was a skilled entertainer and it was a good night. But for the earl, it was Thomas's reputation as a seer which intrigued him most.

In truth, the earl was cynical, and as the evening drew to a close the nobleman sarcastically spoke to Thomas. 'So it is said that ye are a seer, a man who can foretell the future, well, if that be the case, tell us what we can expect for tomorrow!' A wry smile on the earl's face triggered a smattering of muffled mocking laughter amongst some of his guests.

Thomas kept his cool and stared at his host, and then at those who were sniggering. His gaze was like a scythe cutting through corn. It silenced everyone. All eyes were upon him, waiting for his prophesy.

'Tomorrow,' said Thomas, 'will be a day of terrible calamity and misery.' He paused and again scanned the audience with his eyes; he now had their complete attention.

He continued, 'Before the twelfth hour shall be heard a blast so vehement as shall be worse than any before, a blast that shall strike the nations with amazement, shall humble what is proud, and what is fierce shall level to the ground.'

The earl sat unmoved by this prediction of doom, a cynical grin still decorating his face. Then Thomas concluded his prophesy with a low voice, and words spoken slowly: 'It will be the sorest wind and tempest that was ever heard of in Scotland.'

There was no more laughter, just silence, which was broken by the earl. 'So my friends, we had better retire, for as our esteemed seer has told us, we have till noon tomorrow before we are hit with blast and tempest!' Laughter again filled the room.

But not everyone was sure how to react. Although some laughed, others remained silent. But one thing was sure: Thomas had made a dramatic prophesy, and if something very significant didn't happen before noon the next day, then he would be exposed as a fake.

In the morning, the earl looked out of his window. The sound of seabirds now filled the air. The sea was calm after the storm of the previous evening, and the earl shook his head with a smile.

'Well, the wind and tempest seem to have abated,' he said to Thomas, 'perhaps you got the timing wrong, seer.'

'It is not yet the twelfth hour, sire,' replied Thomas.

'Indeed,' nodded the earl, 'let us wait to see if the wind builds to a tempest in the next few hours.'

Thomas remained silent, wandering here and there. Perhaps he was waiting for something to happen, or perhaps he realised he'd got himself into a pickle and was thinking how to get out of it. Noon was fast approaching, and no sign of the prophesised tempest.

The earl called his guests to the table to eat, but mainly so the demise of Thomas could be witnessed by all his guests.

'So it is almost noon, and where is the tempest this so-called soothsayer has said would happen?' All those assembled now mocked Thomas, who remained quiet.

'Let us at least eat heartily, and make a tempest of our own!' proclaimed the earl. Laughter filled the hall.

Just at that moment, a guard rushed in. There was a man at the gate, he said, his horse foaming and sweating from being ridden so hard. The rider yelled that he must see the earl for he had a message of devastating news.

The messenger was brought into the hall, but he could hardly speak for want of breath.

'Terrible news, terrible news,' he said, panting, 'the king is dead.'

A moment's silence was followed by wailing and howls of shock.

'But how is this possible?' asked the earl.

The messenger explained that the king, Alexander III, had fallen from his horse in Fife; a terrible accident that nobody could have foreseen.

Eyes turned to Thomas, who stood to face the now all-believing crowd.

He stood proudly, and vindicated. 'This,' he said with great solemnity, 'is the sore wind and tempest that shall blow through Scotland.'

And indeed it did. The death of Alexander III on 19 March 1286 was to unleash the Wars of Independence, which were the sorest tempest the nation had ever suffered.

This prophesy, made in Dunbar Castle, sealed the reputation of Thomas the Rhymer. The story was recorded by Walter Bower, a chronicler born in Haddington in 1385. He was writing of events more than 100 years before, at a time when tales of Thomas the Rhymer were probably already part of the oral tradition.

The stories and prophesies of Thomas the Rhymer are now part of Scotland's folklore and legends. He may have been from the Borders, but let us not forget he made his mark in the great castle of Dunbar in East Lothian!

10

THE BROWNIE OF BUTTERDEAN WOOD

In a farm close by to Butterdean Wood there lived a brownie. Like all of his ilk, he worked willingly on the farm for small return. The farmer's wife knew this, and would leave a little bowl of creamy milk for him and a wee bit of porridge laced with honey. He didn't want anything else, and was happy with his simple life.

Like all brownies, he was an animal lover. He understood that animals need kindness and love just like people. Perhaps that is why he liked to live in the barn where the animals were kept. But one day, he saw the farmer's son act cruelly to one of the old ponies stabled there. The brownie watched horrified as the pony was struck with a whip, simply because it didn't move fast enough in the son's opinion. The brownie was enraged, and without thinking, he jumped from his hidden corner and shouted at the young man, 'Cease that at aince else I will turn the whip on ye!'

The farmer's son immediately stopped whipping the pony and stared in disbelief at the wee man standing before him. Although the brownie only came up as far as the son's kneecaps, he stood his ground, folding his arms in an angry pose. The son then lifted the whip towards the wee man, who moved very fast, dodging blow after blow, until the son, exhausted and humiliated, finally threw down the whip and left the barn.

After this the brownie decided to leave the farm, but did not want to leave the wee pony for fear that it would once again be subjected to cruelty. And so he took its reins and led it willingly

out of the barn. He took the pony to a field a few miles away, next to Butterdean Wood.

The brownie looked at the wood and realised he could find a place to hide amongst its trees, away from the cruelty of humans. And so he made himself a new home deep within Butterdean Wood, close to an oak tree with three trunks. He would venture out to ensure the pony was well cared for, and it came to him when he whistled. But for most of the time he stayed well away from humans, who now scared and disappointed him.

This was a long time ago, but brownies can live a long time, and folk say he is still there, hiding from cruel and vengeful humans. One day, not so long ago, two young sisters called Mairi and Morvern walked in the wood with their father. They knew the story of the brownie and wanted to show him that not all humans were as cruel and vindictive as that farmer's son.

And so they left some porridge laced with honey as a gift, with a note reassuring him that their intentions were kind. They hoped to see the brownie, and for a moment they thought they did. But they couldn't be sure.

But when they returned to the place they'd left the porridge, it was gone, along with the note.

11

THE WEAVER'S WIFE

Around the time of the last Jacobite rebellion in the eighteenth century, there was a weaver who lived close to North Berwick who loved his wife. This is not to say, of course, that he was the only weaver who loved his wife, or the only man to love his wife. But the truth was that his love for her was so deeply felt and obvious to see that it made other people jealous.

He loved everything about her, and she loved him back just the same. And so, needless to say, they were very happy together. She had a lovely singing voice, and would sing to her husband as he worked.

They had three children together, and when she became pregnant with the fourth child the weaver looked after her as best he could, while also being industrious in his trade in order to provide for his expanding family.

They were poor, yet had enough to be free of the constant cloud of destitution. But then, tragedy struck. The birth of the fourth child was long and agony-laden, and when the child was finally born all eyes were, for a moment, on the child to see if it had survived. To the relief of all it let out a healthy cry. But when the midwife turned to show the child her mother, the poor woman's body lay contorted and lifeless.

Her husband was utterly devastated at the loss of the woman he loved so much. He was inconsolable for a long time. But his grief was made even worse by the gossip that surrounded his wife's death.

The gossip had started at the funeral. Someone in attendance had whispered to a friend, 'That's no his wife's body.'

'Whit dae ye mean?' was the hushed reply from another.

The gossip half covered her mouth with her hands as she said, 'She was taken awa by the wee folk when all een were oan the bairn, she's no deid, she bides wi them noo.'

The gossip eventually reached the ears of the grieving weaver, but he was a God-fearing man, and he did his best to ignore what he believed was superstitious nonsense.

This was the eighteenth century, and belief in the fairies was still widespread in the lowlands despite the efforts of the Church to eradicate it. These were not the fairies we know from Disney movies of course. The wee folk as they were often called, could be dangerous and capricious. A rowan tree, or something made of metal, could keep them away. That is why people put a horseshoe by their door.

Keeping fairies out of your house was important, for it was believed they took things, including babies, substituting them with one of their own, which was often sickly. The fairy substitute was known as a changeling.

But adults as well as babies could be taken by the fairies, and rumours spread that it was a sickly old fairy changeling who'd died, not the weaver's wife. She had been quickly snatched and replaced with a near dead fairy, the gossips said, while everyone was looking at the baby.

Why would the fairies do this? Fairies love beautiful singing, and they may have been smitten by the wife's pure singing voice, and so took the opportunity to steal her away. If this was true, the weaver's wife was still alive, but trapped in fairyland.

But the poor grieving weaver ignored all this silly talk. He was a churchgoer and he knew the soul of his beloved wife was now in heaven. He was in deep grief for a whole year, but then began to realise he must start looking for another wife.

If truth be told, his heart was still hurting and he didn't feel ready to remarry, but he had four children to look after with little in the way of family support. He needed to work to provide for his family and so he lifted himself from his grief and didn't have to look far. He proposed to a neighbour, who was both kindly with the children and a bonny woman in herself.

There was love between them for sure, but deep inside the weaver knew that his departed wife would forever keep a part of his heart, and that he could never truly love any other woman as much as he'd loved her. Yet life has to go on, and he knew he could be content, perhaps even happy, with his new wife, and that she would make a good stepmother to his children.

After she had accepted his proposal, the weaver told the minister, Matthew Reid, so that the bans could be proclaimed. It was perhaps this which brought memories of his beloved departed wife to the fore of his mind that night.

He was lying in bed, unable to sleep, when suddenly a figure entered the room and stood before him. She was dressed in white and looked like his dear departed wife. His heart leapt and he asked her who she was and what did she want.

'Dae ye no recognise me, my dear husband?' she said. The weaver was unable to speak.

'It's me my love, yer dear wife.'

The weaver remained speechless.

'Dinnae fear my love, for I'm no deid. The good neighbours took me, but I'm sair hairted and miss ye and the bairns, I want tae come back tae ye.'

The 'good neighbours', of course, meant the wee folk, or fairies, and she then explained how he could help her escape from them.

'If ye still hae love for me then this is what ye maun dae. Assemble the guid folk o' the toon, with the meenister at the heid, and bring them tae ma grave. Then raise the coffin in which it is said I lie and ask the meenister tae say the Lord's Prayer ower it.

'I will then rise frae the coffin and fly aroond the kirk at muckle speed so ye maun hae a fast runner, such as young William Tait, tae chase and catch me, and then someone tae hud me fast aince I huv bin caught. Ask the smith tae dae this, he is muckle strang. Then, wi the prayers o' the guid folk, I will be restored tae my place in human society an by yer side.'

Suddenly the weaver woke up! It was a dream, but it had been so real he remembered everything his wife had told him. In fact, it was so vivid and clear it did not seem like a dream at all. But, of course, it must have been. So he said nothing of it.

The following night, however, he had the same dream, just as vivid as before, but he again ignored it.

By the third night he was fearful of a repeat experience, and tried to stay awake. As he lay there his wife appeared, but this time she was in a melancholy mood.

'De ye no hae love for me onymair?' she asked him sadly. 'Why dae ye ignore my pleadings? Dae ye no believe it is me my love? If ye dinnae dae as I ask, I will forever be trapped here.'

Then she looked down at the child at whose birth she had supposedly died and picked her up lovingly, and suckled her. Some drops of her milk fell onto his bedclothes.

'Ye see,' she said, 'I am real, please help me.'

He woke up as she left. Then he saw something which struck terror through his body. The stains from the milk were still on his bedclothes! This was now too much to bear, and so he rushed to the minister for advice and help.

The minister listened carefully to what the distressed man said. He knew he was a good member of the congregation, and did not disbelieve his visions.

'I believe all ye say,' said the minister, 'yet I can tell ye that nae being has the power tae detain a Christian soul. What ye hae seen is an illusion frae the deil. It is the Lord who has determined the place o'er your wife's soul.'

The weaver lowered his head as he nodded.

'Besides,' added the minister, 'I cannae order the opening o' a grave and the saying o' prayers ower it, it is a devilish idea, Satan playing tricks.'

The weaver had such mixed emotions. There was a part of him who really wanted to believe that it was true, that the love of his life was still alive and he could rescue her. But he knew the minister was right.

He asked the minister what he should do.

'Get yer new bride's consent tae be marrit tomorrow, or even today if she will agree tae it. I will tak it oan masel tae dispense wi the bans, or will proclaim them three times in ane day. Aince ye hae a new wife, ye will only think o' the former as separated from ye by death, and although ye may hae sad thochts, be also raised by the thocht that she is in heaven.'

And so the weaver took this advice and was married the next day. His first love never again returned to him in a dream, and he grew into happiness with his new wife and they also had children together.

Yet at times, in the darkness of the night, he would wake as if someone had disturbed him. More than once he saw what looked like tear-stains on his sleeve when he woke. And there were also moments, when working, that he was sure he heard a familiar sweet voice singing.

He lived a happy life and loved his second wife. Yet till the day he died, there was a part of him that wondered if his first love was indeed trapped in fairyland, and that he had failed to rescue her.

12

THE FAIRY GLEN

Stories are like seeds blown in the wind, they can travel from one place to another, and set new roots far from their origin. Such is the case with this East Lothian tale, which has its origins in Perthshire, but was replanted here and here this version now belongs.

There is a farm not far from Thurston, which is close to the Fairy Glen in East Lothian. One day, the farmer's wife noticed there had been a change in her husband's behaviour and routine. It was springtime, and there was a lot to do on the farm, yet he seemed to be less than concentrated on the work needed done on the fields. Instead, he would sit for what seemed like ages, humming tunes in his head while chewing on a long grass.

Normally at this time of year he would have been out in the fields all day, or dyking, or repairing the roof. There was evidently lots of work to be done, and the wife herself had her hands full with the bairns, and all that was then considered to be her responsibility. But her husband seemed to have been struck down with a dose of laziness. Sure enough, the farm had provided them with a decent living, but that was partly because of her husband's hard work.

She was worried. 'Whit ails ye dear?' she asked sympathetically, concerned that perhaps he had a pain or illness. But his response was always the same 'Naethin ails me, I'm fine.' But he clearly wasn't fine.

One of the strange things he did was take unusual walks in the evening. He had never done this before, as this had always been a family time, a precious hour or so before bedtime when the family could read or talk after a long, tiring day. But since he'd done less work than usual, the farmer seemed to have extra energy at the tail end of the day, and so he often said, 'I need a walk.' He would wander away and on his return he'd never say where he had been.

One day the wife decided she'd had enough of this. She'd tried talking to him but to no avail. He wouldn't tell her what he was up to on his evening walks, but she felt sure that whatever it was, it was the reason for his changed behaviour. So she would find out.

She got out her spinning wheel and began to spin. She used carefully combed wool, and made a ball of very thin worsted yarn. 'Aye, that'll dae the trick,' she thought to herself.

The next evening, her husband once again said he was off for a walk. 'Aye, alricht dear,' she said, 'but dinnae forget yer jaicket, as there's a wee chill in the air.' She raised his jacket for him and he spread out his arms as she carefully put it on him. Then he left without saying a word.

He hadn't noticed that sewn onto the rim of the jacket at the back was a thread of worsted yarn. His wife held the ball of yarn at the other end. She intended to follow him, but she knew that he would obviously see her if she tried to keep him in sight. This way she could follow him unseen.

The yarn was thin and invisible, yet strong, and it began to unravel in the wife's hands as her husband vanished into the hills beyond. Thankfully, she had made over a mile of it. Suddenly it stopped. Wherever he was, he'd reached his destination.

'What ye daein mither?' asked one of the older children. 'I'm fishing,' she replied. 'Ye look aifter yer wee brothers n sisters, I'm gaun oot tae see whit I've caught.'

And so the gudewife followed the yarn. It didn't lead to the fields, and so it wasn't work that he was doing. Instead it headed for the small valley from which the burn flowed. The slopes got steeper on either side and she had to scramble at some points, scratching herself on the whin, which covered the hillsides with a vivid yellow.

Finally she saw her husband, sitting by the burn talking to a woman! Her footsteps were frozen, as was her heart. The faithless man! While she was working her fingers to the bones, looking after the children, keeping house, feeding his belly, he was dallying with another woman!

She crept closer like a cat to get a better view. How predictable. The woman was young and pretty, very pretty in fact. They held hands, and she kissed him. What could she possibly want with him? No doubt his farm!

Rage built up in the wife's chest and she couldn't help herself. With a great roar, she charged from the whin bush she had been hiding behind. The husband turned to see what the noise was and saw his wife running towards him like a Highlander in a battle charge, screaming and yelling.

'Who's that?' asked the young woman.

'My wife,' said the farmer, and the woman fled the moment he said the words. She skimmed across the burn and into the glen beyond, disappearing like magic into one of the hills, leaving the farmer to take the full brunt of his wife's fury.

She flattened him onto the ground. 'How dare ye!' she said, then burst into tears, as her fury melted into the pain of betrayal.

When they returned to the house, the children were waiting anxiously for them. Their mother's tearstained face told them that something was not right, as did their father's guilty look. But nothing was said. 'Ye bairns gang tae bed, everything's a'richt,' said their father. They looked at their mother for confirmation and she gave it with a nod and forced smile.

And so the husband told his tale. It was a love affair, he had to admit it. He had been enchanted by the woman, not realising at first that she was a fairy woman. He had heard her singing while he was in the glen looking for stones for the dyke. Her singing had enchanted him, and he found himself constantly finding excuses to go there and search her out. Eventually they met, by the fairy hill.

'I have tae admit,' said the farmer, 'that while there wis nae fornication, there was maist certainly a desire fir it oan ma pairt, but ye see, I wis enchanted and bewitched.' She wanted to punch him, but she didn't.

He had been discovered just in time, for he had been ready to go with her into her realm.

'Ye ken how dangerous that is, if ye gang intae their realm ye may mebbe niver come back,' said his wife.

'Aye, my dear, I ken. There's nae fear o' that noo. I think the sicht o' ye charging wi red-faced rage has put the fear o' God intae her, cause the spell is broken, and I'm back tae masel noo.' He begged for forgiveness, and she told him that can't be given, but earned. He understood. Then he looked at her and asked, 'By the way, how did ye ken where I wis?' His wife just smiled and said, 'Maybe I hae magic tae.'

And so the farmer from then on concentrated on his work and his family, glad his wife had forgiven him. Every now and then, a faint sound of singing was carried on a breath of wind from the glen, but he never went back there.

He knew it was dangerous, in more ways than one.

13

A Tale of Two Legends

Those who live by the shore of Prestonpans will tell you of the storms that lash the shoreline there, with waves even drenching the houses close to the sea. It was such a storm, 1,000 years ago, which gave birth to the town.

That storm must have been ferocious, for a sea captain named Althamer had come into the firth to seek calmer waters. It is said he was a pirate, and his name suggests he may have been a Danish Viking. But he had found no shelter from the raging sea, and so searched for a place to land.

Land appeared before him and he yelled to his crew to row with all their might. But as his battered vessel approached the shoreline, Althamer's heart sank. There were rocks everywhere!

He yelled instructions and desperately tried to navigate the boat to avoid the rocks, but the wind was unrelenting and the waves battered the vessel this way and that. Soon they were within a stone's throw of the beach, with chunks of rock appearing and disappearing in the swirling sea.

For a moment, it seemed they would successfully negotiate through the rocks and land on the beach beyond, but a wave lifted the stern and twisted the vessel so its starboard side was ripped by the long edge of a rock shelf.

Men were swept into the sea, as the stricken craft was spun around by another giant wave, throwing Althamer himself overboard. He swallowed a lungful of salt water as he somersaulted upside down under the water. His head scraped against a rock, and he raised his arms to prevent his body being battered.

But as the sea withdrew for a moment, his feet found the ground below him. He was almost ashore, and so with all his strength he waded towards the beach. A wave slammed him from behind, pushing him over and sweeping him forward, and once again his head was submerged in freezing water. But when the sea retreated, he found himself lying on a stony beach.

He dragged himself up, and watched as his boat was minced on the rocks only a few metres away. Some of his men had already reached the beach while others were swirling in the angry waves amongst the wreckage of the boat.

But the waves brought the men ashore. They came sweeping and tumbling with each crash of water. Some were badly hurt, and had to be dragged away before the sea could reclaim them. But eventually Althamer saw all his crew come ashore alive. They had survived the storm, but their boat was utterly destroyed.

The following day, in the calm which follows a storm, amidst the wreckage of their boat, all eyes turned to Althamer. He was their leader: what were they to do now? Build a new boat? Find another one?

'Destiny has brought us to this place,' he told his men, 'so we will stay, and make it our home.' And so they did, and named the village after their leader. Around a hundred years later, when the monks of Newbattle took possession of the land, the small village named Aldhammer was still there. But the new association with the monks led to the village gaining a new name, as it became known as Preiston (meaning priest's town). It began to flourish and became a centre for many industries, including salt panning. And so Preiston's salt pans gave the town the new name of Prestonpans.

But the name of the old pirate is still remembered, as a building called Aldhammer House stands on the very spot where Prestonpans had its ancient beginnings. The house is now modern, but the name is a reminder of the town's legendary founder.

Perhaps it is no coincidence that this rocky birthplace of
Prestonpans is also the site of the town's other ancient legend. Here
sits the great boulder named Johnny Moat. It's a huge 13-tonne oval-
shaped boulder, which settled precariously on the Girdle Rocks. It
is Prestonpans' magic standing stone, brought from far away and
placed there thousands of years ago, not by humans, but by nature.

It was named, it is said, after a harbourmaster of The Haven,
the village's harbour, whose physique and strength resembled the
stone. At high tide only its summit is visible, but at low tide you
can walk to it and sit with it. Legend says it protects the town and
that Prestonpans will flourish, but only if it remains sitting on its
throne.

It is likely that the legendary magic of this ancient boulder
has its roots in the early people's wonder at the sight of it. Maybe
Althamer himself recognised the unusual nature of the stone and
assigned a special role for it. But for nearly 1,000 years, Prestonpans
grew and flourished while Johnny Moat sat on the Girdle Rocks.
Then came the wild storm of December 1952. Johnny Moat was
toppled from its throne, its magic ceased, and Prestonpans went
into steep decline.

One by one, the industries which had made Prestonpans famous
started to close down. The salt pans ceased production, the colliery

closed down, as did the brickworks, the potteries and even the brewery. For forty years Johnny Moat lay like a fallen soldier in the pebbles, unable to protect the town.

But he wasn't forgotten. People noticed how the town had suffered since Johnny Moat had fallen, and many wanted the stone replaced on the Girdle Rocks. But how to lift a 13-tonne boulder? The knights in shining armour were workers laying a new sewage system, who used their machinery on 10 March 1992 to lift Johnny Moat once more onto its rocky throne.

Sadly it was toppled again in 2015 during yet another fierce storm, and despite attempts by locals to find a way to raise it back onto its throne, Johnny Moat remains face down in the sand. If the stone is not raised once again to its rightful position, time will tell what the consequences will be for Prestonpans.

14

THE CRUSOE OF COCKENZIE

It was an autumn day in 1862 when the exotic-looking stranger arrived in the small and close-knit fishing community of Cockenzie. His dress indicated he must be from some faraway place. He wore a hat of French style, and a long coat. His face was clean shaven and bronze, a complexion that suggested he must be from a warmer climate.

As he strolled into the village he studied the houses carefully. He paused at the small cove called the boat shore. It was at this tiny natural harbour that legend tells of the arrival of St Kenneth, who founded the small community that was to become Cockenzie.

The stranger walked on, slowly, looking at every house, but it seemed he was familiar with the place, and explored as if he was reliving old memories.

The progress of this exotic-looking stranger was followed quietly by the eyes of the women. Most of the men were away at the fishing, so the street was dominated by bairns and their mothers.

He then entered a small shop and asked the keeper if a person called Alexander Barbour still lived in the village. He spoke with a local accent, but it was mixed with another less identifiable one.

'Aye, that's his hoose ower there,' directed the shopkeeper.

The man now walked with determined purpose to the house, as if he was excited and had found what he had been looking for. He stood for a moment, nervous, on the doorstep, then knocked on the door.

A woman answered.

'Does Alexander Barbour bide here?' asked the stranger. The woman studied the man, squinted her eyes and slightly turned her head as she cautiously replied.

'Aye, but he's awa at the fishin the noo.'

The man hesitated, as if he had been surprised by the woman's answer. He seemed upset, and stepped away for a moment to compose himself. Then he asked:

'Are ye his wife?'

'Aye, I am,' she replied.

Her answer had an immediate effect on the man. He seemed overtaken with emotion, leant against the doorway and looked down, speaking to himself rather than her; 'Then, my mother is deid.'

Without asking, he entered the house, still distressed. He walked through the house, picking up items, looking at them, casting an

inquisitive eye around the inside of the house. It was as if he had been there before. Then, with tears in his eyes, he sat down.

The woman began to realise who this man may be. She approached him, this time with sympathy.

'Are you …' she asked with breathless anticipation, '… are you Jackie Barbour?'

The man looked up at her.

'Aye, I am.'

'The Lord be praised!' she cried out and her legs were suddenly electrified. She rushed out of the house and into one nearby.

'Yer brother's returned,' she screamed with joy to her husband's daughter, 'he's in the hoose!'

The sister said nothing, but dropped everything and ran into her father's house. She hesitated for a moment in front of him, her eyes welled up with tears. 'It is ye,' she said with a faltering voice, and rushed towards him and wrapped her arms around him in a tight hug, sobbing.

'I kent ye'd come back, I kent it!' she kept on saying.

The stepmother left the two siblings talking and took the opportunity to leave the house to inform the village. Already some neighbours had heard the commotion, and had gathered close-by to find out what was going on.

The stepmum ran through the village, announcing the news that Jackie Barbour had returned! In moments, there were waves of women holding babies heading for the Barbour household, followed by a tide of bairns who wondered what the exciting news was all about and wanted to see for themselves.

The house was mobbed. Some older members of the community shook Jackie's hand, others hugged him. The children had no idea who he was but some shook his hand anyway. The whole village was buzzing with the news of Jackie Barbour's return.

Later, Jackie's father and brother returned from the fishing. They were met by crowds waving and calling out the good news. It was a tear-stained joyful family reunion, and thanks were given at a calmer prayer meeting that Sabbath.

Once the excitement and novelty of Jackie's return had died down, his story began to emerge. He had left the village sixteen years ago on a ship bound for Australia, but then he had vanished. His family were distraught at the lack of news. Sadly, his mother had died believing her youngest son was dead. Only Jackie's sister, who was married to a sailor, had kept the flame of hope alive. She had always believed he was still alive and would one day return.

But what was his story, where had he been in those sixteen years? You can imagine the excited silence as Jackie told his tale to his family:

'I wasnae happy wi ma berth sae I jumped ship. I found myself on a whaler heading for the Pacific. We had the sun richt above us, so we must've been by the equator,' he told them.

'Then one nicht, as maist o' us were sleeping, there wis this almichty crunch. We'd hit rocks. But the waves tossed the ship like a cat playin wi a moose, and she began tae disintegrate.

'I scrambled oot in the darkness, alang wi other crew members. We couldnae see much but could make oot a beach.

'When we got there we just fell doon exhausted. We waited till sunrise in the hope o' salvaging something but the hale ship was already gone! We'd been wrecked oan a heidland, wi a raging tide that'd swept everything awa.

'There were twenty-five o' us, with naething but the ragged claes we were wearing.

'So we decided tae find oot where we were. We reckoned we were oan ane of the Fiji islands, but we didnae ken exactly. We explored the island. There were muckle cliffs in the west but a mair kindly shoreline in the east. Thick forest surrounded it, but strangely there were clearings in the middle o' the island, which we calculated as aboot ten miles in circumference. And, in the middle, there wis a smokin mountain, a volcano.'

Jackie paused in the telling of his tale, and one fascinated listener took the opportunity to ask a question: 'What did ye eat?'

'Weel,' said Jackie, continuing his tale, 'there were many fruit trees, including pineapple, and we found yams under the groond. There were also fruits we didnae ken the name o'. But there werenae many animals and a diet o' fruit soon made us sick. We realised we hud tae catch fish.

'Since I am the son o' a fisherman the duty wis gien tae me, but it wasnae easy without gear. But then we saw something that at first made us feart.'

'What? What wis that?' asked a spellbound listener.

'The island was inhabited. There were aboot six hundred o' them, and they caught their fish wi simple spears. Sae we did the same.

'We had nothing tae dae with them. They were a godless race, wearing nae claes, and talking tae the trees.

'But there was also a respect atween us. They sometimes gied us gifts o' fish. They showed us how tae cook the yams in the embers o' the volcano. We wud cook the fish likewise.

'But the worst o' it was the boredom. We hadnae even a Bible tae read. Sae we telt each ither stories. We got tae ken each ither's lives as if they were oor ain. But death was ay in the shadows. We stairted dying. After some time there were only thirteen o' us, wi twelve graves reminding us that we were once twenty-five.

'We spent hours looking at the horizon fir rescue. We were going crazy. There were fechts, and worse. We wore oor ragged claes, not because we had tae but tae show we still had Godly civility within us despite oor desperate condition.

'I can tell ye I prayed every day, I dreamt o' Cokenny and the cool lapping shore, the sound o' women and bairns and the feeling o' bein at hame. I felt sure I wouldnae ever see Cokenny agin, that my grave would also be oan that godforsaken island and that my family would never ken where I rested.

'Years passed but we couldnae tell how many years we had spent stranded oan the island. I felt my body failing, and I was close tae death when I heard the screaming: "A ship a ship, we are delivered, praised be tae God!" I wasnae sure if I was dreaming it, and I fell intae a slumber.

'Then I awoke aboard a schooner called the *Irish Girl*. We were already at sea headed fir California. I can tell ye, I cannae say in words the joy I felt then. Ma body came back tae me, ma strength and ma spirit returned, and I hud just one desire, tae be back in Cokenny wi my family.

'I discovered we hud spent nine years oan that island, yet it felt like fifty. It took me near two years working in California to raise enough funds tae begin my journey hame but …' Jackie's voice broke with emotion for a moment, 'but noo, I'm hame.'

And so he was, and lived there, by the shore he'd often dreamt of, for the rest of his life.

15

A Salty Tale from Cockenzie

Sandy Hewit lived around 200 years ago and worked in Cockenzie's salt pans. Yet according to local historian Alex Hamilton this was not the only way he made his living, as he also moonlighted as a smuggler. In those days, salt was heavily taxed so money was to be made if the tax could be avoided. To do so was of course illegal, and it was the job of the gauger to keep a very careful eye on the movement of salt from the sealed girnels. Sandy has been called the 'most accomplished salt smuggler that ever plied the trade at Cockenzie'. His cat-and-mouse exploits with the customs men have left many local tales.

He mostly worked alone, but did sometimes use accomplices. On one occasion, a gauger was approaching where Sandy was working and noticed a bag of salt standing in a corner, obviously ready for dispatch.

Suddenly Sandy started to look shifty, and turned to an assistant and whispered, 'Ye ken whit tae dae wi it.' The assistant quickly took the bag of salt into the works while Sandy attempted to engage the gauger in small talk.

'It's a braw day, dae ye na think?'

'Dianne tak me fir a fool Sandy, when ye stop me tae talk aboot the weather I ken whit yer up tae.'

The gauger rushed into the salt works just in time to see the bag of salt being hauled out of an airhole in the roof. Like lightning, the gauger rushed outside and round the building, sure this time he had caught the sleekit Sandy.

But there was no evidence of the bag! The gauger wasn't going to give up, and so he returned to speak to Sandy. He was clearing red-hot cinders from the furnace onto a flagstone on the floor. 'Watch yerself, gauger, them cinders are gye hot tae be staundin oan,' he said.

'I ken yer up tae something, Sandy,' replied the gauger.

'Aye, I am, as ye can see, I'm clearing the furnace, and while you're standing there watching me, that lad will be skirting ower the rocks wi that bag o' salt oan his back, cause he can run faster than a hare.'

The gauger, thinking himself outwitted, immediately ran out and across the rocks in an attempt to catch the lad red-handed. Sandy then carefully cleared the red-hot cinders from the flagstone. He usually stood there when working by the furnace, and for good reason. Satisfied that the gauger was out of sight, Sandy carefully lifted the flagstone, under which was the bag of salt, plus a number of others, all ready to be smuggled away.

As the gauger had run round the outside of the building, the bag had been quickly lowered back and concealed under the flagstone, just in time. Sandy was covering the evidence with the cinders as the gauger walked in.

But how did he manage to dispatch the illicit bags of salt?

Some in Cockenzie say a tunnel was revealed in a storm some years ago by the boat shore, it led to somewhere in the village.

Maybe to a flagstone floor? Some say it leads to the grounds of Cockenzie House itself.

Maybe Sandy Hewit wasn't the most successful salt smuggler of Cockenzie after all, maybe it was someone much higher up the social scale? The rich and powerful involved in illegal activities?

Surely not!

A tale told by Alex Hamilton and Mags Nisbet Macfarlane.

16

BLEEZING FOU AT CANTY BAY

On a calm day on the third Sabbath of July 1822, a drama unfolded at sea by the shoreline at Castleton, just beyond Canty Bay. A shot rang out as a lugger was being pursued by a cutter. The lugger had been in the area for a couple of days and had been noticed by many locals. But it had also drawn the attention of the customs men, for it was suspected that the lugger was involved in smuggling. The customs men in the cutter were now in hot pursuit in what was becoming a cat-and-mouse chase at sea, for the lugger was indeed full of brandy kegs.

The smugglers were manoeuvring wildly in a desperate attempt to escape, and as they neared the shore they began to throw the kegs into the sea. Soon the sea was full of half submerged and sinking kegs. The tactic worked: it distracted the pursing cutter for a few vital moments, just long enough to allow the now lighter and faster lugger to make a dash for the open sea.

It was quite a spectacle, and one of those witnessing it was John Whitecross, a tenant at Canty Bay. He watched as the cutter chased the smugglers out into the North Sea, but to no avail. It seemed to vanish and reappear like magic, because it was painted different colours on each side. Finally, the smuggler's vessel vanished completely, leaving the customs men to limp back red-faced and empty-handed.

But now there was a new crop to be harvested at the shore. As the tide went out, it revealed a shoreline peppered with kegs. John wasted no time in organising his men. It was unfortunately still the Sabbath, but this wasn't really work, was it?

Time was of the essence, as for sure the customs men would soon arrive to retrieve the kegs before the tide turned. Small boats steered the coastline, fishing the kegs that still bobbed below the surface, while carts by the shore were taken onto the beach for the harvest. Soon they were piled high with brandy kegs. It was a collective community effort, with women and children willingly conscripted into the task.

But it was dangerous, as the customs men could arrive at any time. So John sent some of the children to act as lookouts while the business of hiding the kegs was organised. One of those involved was George Hogg, the grieve at Castleton. He supervised the exercise with military precision. He was well used to it, as everyone knew he had regular dealings with the smugglers.

'Tak thae kegs and put them in the mill,' he instructed farmhands. The windmill was just beyond the shoreline. He chose the two strongest lads for the job, as they carried two kegs each, one under each arm. They got there just in time.

'The gaugers! The gaugers are here!' cried two boys as they ran from their look-out point.

Too late, it seemed. The customs men had spotted the two hinds coming out of the windmill and they immediately headed for it.

'Ye'll no find onything in there, sirs,' said George but they pushed their way inside. But as they searched, George unlocked the 'wings' of the mill. Suddenly the thrashing machinery began working without supervision and the customs men decided it was too dangerous to continue.

They came out and squared up to George in a threatening pose. 'We ken yer hiding them, and when we find them, yer gangin tae jail.' George kept his cool, and just shrugged his shoulders. The customs men headed off to search the area.

Kegs were concealed everywhere. They had been hidden in folk's houses, concealed in barns and camouflaged in hollows and cracks in the rocks. As the gaugers searched people's homes, they discovered a wave of illness seemed to have hit the area, as many of the wives had taken to bed. Under the sheets were kegs in positions too delicate for any customs man to search.

One customs man, fully aware of what the bump under the bedcovers really was, asked the woman, 'Whit's that under yer blanket?'

'It's ma leg,' she replied, pretending to be ill.

He studied it, then looked at her. 'Fir sure, I havnae seen sic a muckle swelling as that, yer husband maun sleep oan the flair.'

'Weel,' she replied, 'the nicht he may dae just that!'

One of the tenants at Castleton was Mr Robertson. He was a God-fearing man and disapproved of smuggling as a sin. He kept out of it, yet he knew many of his neighbours were involved. But he took a blind eye to it and wasn't going to inform on them. 'The Lord kens a',' he would say to his wife, 'as lang as we keep tae Scripture we hae nae fear.'

But now, amidst all this frenzy, one of his desperate neighbours asked him to hide two kegs. The pious Robertson, of course, at first refused, but the desperation of his neighbour was great.

'The gaugers are here noo,' he said, 'I hae nae time tae hide them, and if caught ma bairns will suffer. Are we no commandit tae love oor neebours as oorsels?' This was too much, and so the kind-hearted Robertson gave in to this pressure and, against his principles, agreed to hide the kegs in his house.

He hid them in a large box just in time, for there was a loud knock at his door. Two customs men stood on his doorstep. The customs men knew Robertson was one of the few who would never get involved, but they had a duty to ask at every door.

'We are oan his majesty's business, as ye ken. Hae ye ony ...' The customs men hadn't finished before Robertson interrupted with his admission.

'Aye aye, may the Lord forgie me, I hae twa kegs, there're in that box,' he said, pointing to it. The customs men seemed surprised then entered the house and examined the box. Sure enough, the kegs were there. They carried them from the house, and the nervous Robertson stood ashamed with his wife as they walked past.

After the gaugers had left, the Robertsons were racked with guilt and remorse. How could they have let themselves, and God, down in such a manner? They prayed for forgiveness. Then, later on, there was another knock on the door. It was the two customs men. They had returned, Mr Robertson assumed, to arrest him. But no!

'These belong tae you, I believe,' said one of them, and they walked away leaving the two kegs on the doorstep.

'Is it a trick?' asked Roberson's wife. 'I dinnae ken whit tae make o' this,' replied her husband. But he got the answer from George Hogg.

'They couldnae find any o' the ither kegs, so it is better fir them tae say that none exist rather than admit failure tae their superiors. They will tell them that nothing was landed.'

'Besides,' added John Whitecross, 'one of the gaugers is a smuggler himself, so he doesnae want onybody sniffing aroond here until he has his kegs awa!'

That night, the inhabitants around Canty Bay and Castleton were all 'bleezing fou'. In fact, the party lasted quite a while, so Canty Bay certainly lived up to its name!

And even the Robertsons could join in. They had a free conscience, as they believed that God had rewarded their honesty with two kegs of fine brandy! And so it would most certainly be sacrilegious not to drink them!

17

COCKLES BRAE

Cockles Brae is part of the road which runs to the south of Haddington, and was one of the routes taken by fishwives as they carried their heavily laden creels to Gifford. It's not a terribly steep brae, but it's quite long and anyone who has walked up the brae will attest that getting to the summit is good exercise!

Many years ago, an elderly fishwife trod this route for the last time. The sweat began to glisten on her forehead as she walked up the hill towards Gifford. She was carrying a creel of cockles, and clasped in her hands were strands of barley and wild flowers. She had already walked many miles from her village on the coast, and there was still a way to go.

She was a fishwife, but also a mother and grandmother, and she carried the livelihood of her family on her back. In the days of her youth she would have been singing to herself on such a fine sunny day, but now she was far from those times and her bones ached with the burden she carried.

She paused for a moment as the road beyond her rose towards Gifford. She was following her own well-worn footsteps and she knew that the brae ahead, while not very steep, was long and weary.

She wore the traditional fishwives' costume, and she had always worn it with pride. On this day, however, the heat bore down on her and her clothes were not ideal. She tilted her head down, in a bent posture, and summoned up all her energy as she began to walk up the brae.

She knew she could not dally, the heat would rot her produce if she didn't get to her customers in good time. She muttered under

her breath as she strove ahead, cursing the heat, her aches and the weight of the creel.

Then she stopped. A wave of nausea had come over her and so she decided to rest. She walked over to a tree on the edge of the road, and there she rested the creel on the far side of the tree trunk out of the sun, and she sat down.

She felt strange and unusual. Thoughts of her family ran through her mind, and old memories danced in her imagination. Then she could feel her body well up inside. There was something wrong, a strange pain suddenly gripped her and a blanket of darkness covered her as she curled up then lay on the ground.

Thus the life of this hard-working woman came to an end at the base of the brae she had so often travelled.

It wasn't long before a passer-by realised that she was not just resting in the sunshine. Word was quickly sent to her community, and friends and family arrived to bring her body home for burial.

However, her creel, full of cockles, went unnoticed in all the commotion. She had carefully placed it in the shade, unseen from the road. And there it remained after her body had been taken home. A curious passing creature may have helped tip the basket and spill the contents, which quickly rotted in the heat.

The following day, two men were on their way to Haddington from Gifford. As they approached the base of the brae, an almighty smell assaulted them.

'Och, whit a stench!' said one of the men, holding his nose.

'It's comin frae ower there,' said his companion, who went to investigate. As he approached the tree the smell grew stronger. Flies were buzzing around a pile of rotten, stinking cockles. At first, he couldn't understand how this could be, but then he saw the creel lying on its side. There were rotten cockles spewed all around, the source of the horrible smell.

Who had the job of removing the creel and its minging contents is not recorded, but the memory of the smell lingered much longer than the smell itself. So ever since, that section of the road became known as Cockles Brae.

18

THE RED SKIPPER OF DUNBAR

Let us begin this tale with the moment two young people fell in love. It was Dunbar in 1760, and Annie Hunter and Tom Hamilton were head over heels in love with each other.

As was the custom in those days, Tom visited Annie's father to ask for her hand in marriage. He was very agreeable to this, for Tom was the son of the provost. Annie's father was a town councillor, or Baillie, and he was happy to see his daughter married to Tom because it was obviously to his advantage. Sadly, he was a man with little fatherly love, and his daughter knew it. Yet in this marriage proposal everyone could be happy!

Just as the Baillie was about to agree to Tom's request, the door opened and a man entered the room uninvited. He stood menacingly for a moment, dressed in what appeared to be clothes from an earlier century. 'No, Baillie,' he said, 'your daughter is mine, ye promised her hand tae me eighteen years ago.'

Both Tom and the Baillie laughed at such nonsense.

'She is nae lang past her eighteenth birthday, so whoever ye are leave this hoose and tak yer nonsense wi ye. She is tae marry me, for she loves me,' said Tom.

But the man walked further into the room and looked straight at the Baillie.

'Hae ye forgotten the incident at yer daughter's christening?'

The Baillie stopped laughing.

'Aye, that's richt, ye remember me noo, I'm the Red Skipper, and ye made me a promise.'

Tom looked at the Baillie for an explanation, but was not reassured by his look of fear. It was as if he'd been visited by a ghost.

'Who is this man, what is he talking aboot?' asked Tom, now worried and anxious.

The Baillie sat down and told of what had happened eighteen years before.

'Aye, it's true,' said the Baillie, 'wee Annie had just been christened and me and her mother were takin her hame on the cairt, when fir a moment we fell asleep. When we woke, this man was holding her, and he only gaed her back after we'd promised her tae him. We thocht it was a joke.'

'I wis nae joke,' said the Red Skipper menacingly.

Tom stepped forward, eyeing the man. 'I dinnae care, I love Annie as she does me and we will marry. Who are ye anyway?'

'I am the Red Skipper,' said the stranger.

'That means nothing, unless you can tell me who is your kin, be awa wi ye!'

The skipper chewed his lip for a moment and slowly nodded his head.

'Aye, very weel, I'll go, but…' he looked at the Baillie, 'ye have broken yer word, sae beware.'

Shivers chilled the Baillie's spine.

Just at that moment Annie appeared, having heard what was going on. She clung to Tom nervously.

'Dinnae let him tak me,' she pleaded.

'On my life, to reach ye he will hae to cut through my body,' said Tom.

The Red Skipper stepped slowly backwards, saying nothing with words but oozing menace. Tom watched him leave and walk away into the high street, then in the blink of an eye he seemed to vanish.

The two men sighed with relief. They returned to the topic of marriage, and Annie smiled at Tom as he repeated his request to her father for her hand in marriage. It was only for moments he took his gaze away from her, to hear her father's answer. But in those moments, somehow she was snatched.

Her cries for help were quickly muffled and she was suddenly gone. Tom ran into the street with the Baillie, calling Annie's name. They searched everywhere, but to no avail. Tom was demented, and in desperation searched every yard of the rocky coast between Dunbar and North Berwick over the next couple of days.

Then he began to search the coast south-east of Dunbar, something in his instinct began to tell him this was where the Red Skipper had his hideout. He searched like a madman, along the rocky coast as far as Fast Castle. Determination was giving way to despair when he saw something caught on the edge of a rock, flapping in the wind.

He scrambled towards it, his heart racing. It was a laced kerchief, and Tom knew it to be Annie's. His eyes scoured the coastline like an eagle. There were caves here, he wanted to call out his Annie's name, but sense stopped him. If she was captive here then he would just warn her captives. Besides, it was getting dark. He must return to get help.

He rushed back to Dunbar, clutching the kerchief. When he arrived at the house of Annie's father in Shore Wynd, he entered without knocking, keen to share his news. But the sound of talking stopped him in his tracks. He stood in the corridor outside and listened. The voices were unmistakable; they were those of Annie's father and the Red Skipper.

He crept as close to the door as he dared and listened over the beating of his heart.

The Red Skipper spoke firmly: 'Consent tae the marriage and I will mak ye a wealthy man, I assure ye, ye dinnae want tae refuse the like's o' me.'

'But what o' Tom?' asked the Baillie.

'Leave him tae me, he will be deid by morning.'

'Aye, that will stop him asking questions,' said the Baillie, and then asked, 'Twa hunner poonds, ye say? It's a deal.'

Tom had no time to be horrified by what he'd heard. He knew the Baillie kept pistols in a side room, and in a moment he was entering the room with two loaded weapons. But there were three men in the room, as the Skipper had brought one of his thugs with him.

For a moment Tom stood, hands shaking, not with fear but rage. 'One bullet is maist definitely for ye,' he said to Annie's treacherous father. He cowered behind the Red Skipper, who didn't flinch.

'Ye'd be better takin oot masel an ma man, fir this cowerin worthless wretch cud easily be dealt wi by Annie herself,' said the Red Skipper, as he pushed the cowardly Baillie down onto the floor in front of Tom.

Then suddenly it was dark. The third man had blown out the candles. There was the sound of scuffling feet, then a punch to Tom's head followed. He could not see but fired his pistols into the darkness. A groan told him at least one shot had found its mark, but soon silence followed.

Tom's eyes adjusted to the dim light and he could see all three were gone, and the door was locked on the outside. He banged it with all his might, and somebody unbolted it. When the door opened, Annie's father stood before him, all apologetic and pleading forgiveness. Tom had no time for this worthless man, he rushed to tell his trusted friends the story and assemble a party to search the caves at sunrise.

The sea was angry that morning, and the search of the rocky crevices below the cliffs took all day. Tom's friends were as determined as he to find the hideout. For sure this was a smugglers' coastline, for they discovered much evidence of their activities. Yet it was close to sunset before they finally came across an entrance that roused their suspicions.

It was pitch dark inside, so they proceeded very carefully. The roar of the waves echoed in the cave's belly, but Tom had a sense they were on the right track.

Then suddenly standing before Tom was Annie. She was pale, her eyes seared with terror, and a glint of radiance surrounded her.

She pointed at the entrance to the next cave, 'Beware my love, there lies treachery.'

Tom couldn't speak for joy but ran towards her. He found himself embracing cold air. His joy drained from him. It had not been his beloved Annie, but a ghostly apparition.

But his friends had seen and heard her too. 'She came to warn us,' said one.

Now with great care, Tom and his friends entered the next cave. Tom clutched his pistol tightly. His friend headed in first, holding up a lantern. What he saw made him recoil and rush back to Tom.

'Dinnae go in there Tom, for God's sake, dinnae go in.'

But Tom snatched the lantern and rushed into the darkness, and the sight that awaited him made him fall to his knees in unimaginable grief. He let out a wail of emotional pain which echoed round the cave.

Tom hugged Annie's lifeless body, sobbing from his soul. Then an evil laughter echoed in the chamber.

Tom lifted the lantern and in the flickering light he saw four men, one of them the Red Skipper. They stood across a chasm, with the boiling tide running between them. They were laughing at his grief.

Tom's grief was eclipsed with rage and vengeance, and he flew across the rocks like a wildcat. But the chasm was wide and he landed on the sharp rocks lying spreadeagled at the Red Skipper's feet. With lightning speed he grabbed the Red Skipper's ankle.

The grief and rage within Tom gave him superhuman strength, and he lifted the Red Skipper and spun him round, bringing his head down onto the sharp rocks, splitting his head and killing him instantly. Tom then despatched the other three with similar superhuman rage. Then his grief overwhelmed him.

'Annie,' he said, 'ye crossed the rivers o' death tae save me. I have avenged you, but noo I will join ye.'

'No Tom, no!' his friends called out, but it was too late. Tom threw himself into the boiling sea. For a split moment, his friends saw him amidst the foam and waves. Then he vanished.

Tom and Annie were finally united, forever.

19

THE OLD SAILOR OF TANTALLON

Those who have yet to see Tantallon Castle will be unprepared for the sense of awe its location and setting will inspire. This massive ruin, perched atop a dramatic cliff, with the crashing sea below, is the stuff of imagination. But it's real!

The traditional rhyme 'Ding doon Tantallon, mak a brig tae the Bass' reflects the belief that both events are considered an equally impossible challenge. Yet Tantallon was finally dinged doon by the cannonballs of Cromwell's troops in 1651, and the once proud home of Douglas earls and dukes was left a ruin. But what a massive, spine-tingling ruin it is! And a homeless sailor was possibly the last human resident of this magnificent medieval castle.

This sailor had fallen on rocky times, literally. The rocky Isle of Fidra had put an end to his seafaring days. Shipwrecked and destitute at the beginning of the nineteenth century, this old sailor made an attempt to start a new life.

But this was not easy. Times were hard and only unfamiliar work on the land available. What was worse, he could find no permanent place to live. Then, while he was searching for loose tatties in a field, he saw the huge silhouette of Tantallon Castle.

It was less the romantic image of the place he was interested in, but rather the possibility he might find a place to shelter within its extensive ruins. The sailor knew nothing of the castle's history, but knew at one time it must have been a magnificent residence.

And so he investigated the ruins carefully, examining every nook and cranny for a potential hideaway he could live in. At one point, as he climbed up a dark stairway, he paused as he heard a strange noise. He listened intently. What was it?

It was the wind, he was sure it was the wind. And so he continued his search. He reached a narrow turnpike stair, and at the top he eventually discovered the remains of a chamber beyond a ruined set of steps. It was hidden from view, and quite a scramble to reach, and so not a place any casual visitor to the ruins would notice.

'This would be perfect,' he thought to himself, and he climbed up the ruined walls into the chamber. It was wind tight, cosy even, but with ample space. And so without delay he moved in! It provided him with a place to sleep out of the wind and rain. Finally he had a home, although it was lonely up there all by himself. He was used to company, and craved companionship.

Then one day, he was on his way back to his noble residence when he came across another unfortunate man who was likewise homeless. So the sailor invited him to stay. Soon there was a small group of destitute people living in the upper chamber, where once nobles like 'Bell the Cat' had resided. The hideout was well hidden, and entered by a rope ladder which could be pulled up and kept out of sight.

The sailor and his companions would hide and sleep during the day and venture out in the evening when nobody would dare go near the dark ruins. It seemed a perfect place to snuggle in for the winter. The locals were convinced the ruins were haunted, so this meant most people kept away from them.

Then one day, a group of young women were working in a field near to the castle, thinning turnips. Suddenly one of them let out a scream!

'Look,' she said, 'up there, someone is watching us from the castle.'

'Och, nonsense, it's been deserted for a hunner and fifty years,' said one of the other girls.

'Maybe ye saw a ghaist,' joked another.

'I'm telling ye, there's someone up there,' the lass insisted.

The girls were now spooked, and peered at the castle walls. Sure enough, a head popped out and quickly disappeared again.

That was it. They ran screaming towards North Berwick and raised the alarm.

In no time, a posse of young lads from North Berwick arrived and began to search the ruins. Yelling and shouting, they finally discovered the old sailor hiding in his chamber. His roommates, it seems, had managed to flee just in time, leaving him alone once again.

The poor terrified sailor was roughly dragged from his hideout and marched into town. He was thrown into jail, and after languishing there while awaiting trial he was banished from the district. But what was his crime?

Well, locals reported that things had gone missing. One local resident had reported his clothes had been stolen, another said food had been taken from his larder. Sheep had also mysteriously vanished.

There was no evidence the old sailor was responsible for any of these crimes, yet his destitute state was considered proof enough that he must have taken part in such activities.

And so he was banished from the area forever. He left, perhaps casting a last glance at the ancient ruins of Tantallon, which for a while were his home.

He never returned, and where he went and what happened to this last resident of Tantallon Castle we will never know.

20

CLACK, CLACK, CLACK

The year 1306 was a tumultuous one in Scottish history, and one dark night in this year a sentry was pacing on the battlements of the old Fa'side Castle keeping watch. He was suddenly startled by the sound of horses galloping, and this was then followed by a shout. He peered down into the darkness but could see nothing.

His heart pounding, he moved along the battlements to the point above the entrance and held out his torch into the dark, cold air, screwing up his eyes to see if anyone was at the gate. But he could see nothing.

He then hurried to the guardroom to ask the others if they had heard anything. But when he entered the room he caught his fellow guards snoozing on duty. They were annoyed at being woken, but insisted that they hadn't really been asleep and had heard nothing. The sentry returned to his post, baffled and wondering if he'd just imagined it all.

But no sooner had he returned to his post than another eerie noise disturbed his senses. The night was cold and still, and the sound he heard was crisp and clear: *clack, clack, clack*. He turned his head, listening intensely to identify the source of the noise. 'It can't be,' he muttered under his breath. It was coming from a turret on the west of the castle, which he knew had been unused for many years.

He stood motionless for some time, listening to the strange noise. What could this strange sound be, a trapped bird perhaps? No, it was a regular rhythmic sound, as if someone was working or making something. But who would be working at this time of night? And who would be in that cold disused part of the castle anyway?

And so he approached the door to the chamber and put his ear to it. *Clack, clack, clack*, the noise continued. He threw open the old studded door and a waft of cold air fanned his torch, making it momentarily burn brighter, flooding the old chamber with light.

An old woman was spinning in the room. She stopped her work and looked up at the shocked sentry. His torch began to flicker and the flame dimmed, and darkness filled the room once again. He stood terrified, but what had caused his terror was not the sight of the old woman.

As she had looked up at him, the sentry had noticed something else, something which had caused his terror. He had seen the metal bars of the grated window behind her. They glistened for a moment in the flame. But he saw them *through* the woman's body.

In that moment, he realised she was a ghost!

The sentry's breathless explanation to the fellow guards was not believed. But his terror and shock seemed genuine. So they agreed to accompany him back to the turret to investigate. But there was no sign of the old woman or her spinning wheel. The other guards laughed and scoffed, but the sentry knew what he'd seen and kept to his story.

The following evening, just as the sun was going down, the sound of galloping hooves was heard once again. This time a rider did arrive at the castle. He called out desperately for the gates to be opened. He had terrible news. The brave Sir Christopher Seton had been executed, hanged by the forces of Edward I.

The sentry's tale was told and retold, and then eventually half-forgotten and the old castle was replaced by another one.

Then in 1513, the spinner was heard again. *Clack, clack, clack*, came from a turret. This time it foretold the untimely death of another Seton at the Battle of Flodden.

The chamber no longer exists, but according to the legend the old woman in her steeple-crowned hat still waits in the castle, her spinning wheel silent, until another untimely death needs to be announced.

And once that time comes, the sound of her working will be heard once again: *clack, clack, clack*.

21

WEE SHORT-HOGGERS OF WHITTINGHAME

Nobody saw her as she huddled secretly under the trees. She had managed to find a place in the wood away from the road, and from the fields. The pains in her body were near unbearable as she knelt, gripping the ground and doing her best to muffle her screams of pain.

She knew she must give birth as silently as possible, she must not be discovered. It was her shame to bear and she'd concealed it for nine months. The man whom she had loved and trusted had disowned her. He was free just to walk away and have nothing more to do with her.

But as the child grew inside her, she knew that because she was unmarried she faced public humiliation and rejection. And so she had concealed the evidence of what she was made to believe was her sin.

It hadn't been easy. She'd worn extra clothing to fool suspicious eyes. She'd worked in the fields as usual. Even still, she was sure some suspected. And now her baby was coming. If she was heard, then all would have been in vain, her life would be ruined. She was in a desperate situation, and her desperation gave her the strength to hide her cries.

And there, under the arching embrace of an old oak tree, she gave birth to her wee baby boy. She cradled him, but he began to cry. She wrapped him tightly in her shawl, rocking to and fro, singing him a lullaby. His mother's tears streamed down her face and fell onto his head, baptising him.

Then a new pain gripped her body. It wasn't a physical pain, but she felt it nonetheless. The trees and birds were the only witnesses to her agony. Soon her son had stopped crying. She let out a howl of grief and guilt, yet it was a silent scream, except within her soul. She carefully unfurled her tiny son from her arms, and kissed him on his forehead. Then she lay his naked and lifeless body on the ground.

She dug furiously with her hands, finding a place between the roots of the tree where her son could rest. And there she lay him, in a cradle of earth. She knelt over him, saying a prayer, asking God to forgive her and pleading that her child be accepted into heaven.

And then in a frenzy she covered him with soil and dirt, with a blanket of leaves and twigs to hide his presence.

She stood and wiped her face. It was done. She now had to return to the fields, and pretend nothing had happened. It was vital she didn't return here, for she could be found out. She must be strong.

In all this she forgot one thing. She forgot to give her son a name.

It was a few years after this that the weeping was first heard. It came from the woods between the kirk and the fields. It was the crying of a young child, but no child was seen.

Then, one evening, it was heard on the road to Stenton. It was the ghostly sound of a young boy crying. Soon afterwards, some farmhands heard the wailing and to their horror they saw a ghostly apparition of a young boy sitting on a wall on the edge of the wood.

He was weeping and holding his head in his hands.

The ghostly young lad threatened nobody, but his presence in the neighbourhood caused people to feel afraid. They would run from him or change direction as soon as they heard or saw him. One person at least knew who this distraught spirit was, but she dared not tell.

It was, of course, the spirit of the wee boy laid to rest in the woods of Whittinghame. His soul could not enter heaven, for he had no name. And so the wee lad's spirit was condemned to wander the woods and lanes of Whittinghame, lamenting his nameless state.

And then, one morning, a local 'drunken blellum' was staggering along the road. He zigzagged along the path, as the alcohol was still affecting his ability to walk straight. He sang an undecipherable tune to himself, and was not too drunk to notice the pleasant morning air, and enjoy the sunrise.

Then he suddenly saw the ghost of the wee nameless boy sitting on a wall, looking forlorn and sad. The drunk man stopped and stared at the wee ghost. As he stood, he swayed to and fro as if about to fall flat his face. But he was studying the sad face on the boy, and felt for him. He noticed the boy had bare feet and the way the shadow was falling upon him made it look like he was wearing footless stockings.

And so the drunk man raised his arms and his voice, and called out cheerfully, 'Hoo's a' wi ye this morning, Short Hoggers?' In an instant the wee ghost's demeanour changed. Someone had actually talked to him, and what's more, had given him a name.

The wee ghost jumped for joy. Now he finally had a name! He leaped off the wall and skipped away, calling out happily to himself, 'Oh weel's me noo! I've gotten a name. They ca me Short-Hoggers o' Whittinghame!'

And so it must be assumed that this name was accepted for entry into the other world, for after his encounter with the kindly drunk man, the wee ghost was never seen again.

22

THE HAUNTED HOUSE

East Lothian has so many ghostly tales to choose from, but there is one place in our county that perhaps has more tales of ghosts than anywhere else: the 400-year-old Penkaet Castle, also known as Fountainhall.

It is a lovely old building, added to and developed over the centuries, and full of Scots architectural character. But it seems to have attracted ghosts in quite a number.

One of the ghosts was of a man called Alexander Hamilton, who was a homeless beggar, living a miserable hand to mouth existence. He lived by begging and could at times be aggressive if refused. He could be forgiven this, as it's not easy to be cheerful and happy when suffering from hunger and destitution. But people would tire of him and so he was constantly moved on from one place to another.

One day he was passing the grand Penkaet Castle. 'Fir sure, the folk biding in sic a grand hoose will hae some scraps they can spare, just a wee bit tae gie me,' he said to himself.

So he walked up the drive and knocked on the front door. Perhaps this was his mistake. If he had gone to the servants' entrance he would have been more warmly welcomed. But when the door opened the lady of the house, and her daughter, stood before him.

Alexander touched his forehead in respect and asked if he could have a small something to help him on his way. He was dirty and smelly, very unkempt looking. Lady Ormiston was angry and had little time for him. She ordered him to immediately leave.

In desperation, Alexander begged yet again: 'I am sure that ye folk wha bide in such a muckle hoose maun hae a wee scrap or twa fir an unfortunate hameless man like masel.'

But this just had the opposite to the desired effect. The daughter's anger was raised. How dare such a scruffy and unkempt man come to the front door and beg! And so Alexander was thrown off the property.

But he didn't leave without protest. As Lady Ormiston and her daughter closed the door on him, Alexander stood, raised his hands and cried out, 'I curse ye baith fir yer cruel and uncommonly attitude tae a beggar, may ye ken yerselves whit it is tae suffer.' The door closed on him and he was escorted roughly from the property.

Only two days later, Lady Ormiston woke with a pain in her stomach. She developed a fever with painful cramps, and a doctor was called. Her eldest daughter, the one who had been with her on the doorstep two days previously, also developed the same mystery illness. Their fever raged as the pain intensified, and soon both were dead.

Then the servants remembered the words of the beggar's curse: 'May ye ken yerselves whit it is tae suffer!'

This could only be witchcraft! And so the hunt for Alexander Hamilton was on. The poor homeless man was found sleeping in a derelict barn. He was terribly beaten and dragged away to Edinburgh for trial.

A servant gave testimony that she saw Alexander tie blue string to the doors as part of his spell. Alexander admitted to this under torture. Well, he would have admitted anything under torture, as all of us would have.

And so the poor, innocent man was hanged.

The next day, a servant was cleaning a window at Penkaet and shrieked. Others came running. 'There,' she said, pointing at the doors of the house, 'the beggar, he was there!' They saw nothing at that moment, but soon after he was seen again, waiting at the door, a ghostly apparition, unkempt and scruffy. And was seen many times thereafter.

Perhaps Alexander Hamilton's ghost used to invite others into the house, for other spirits have been seen inside the building. One of them was the ghost of John Cockburn, who was seen walking out of a cupboard and across the room into a wall! Yet another terrifying vision appeared to Sir Andrew Lauder when he was a young boy. He was exploring the upper levels of the house and saw a ghost standing by a fireplace!

And so, by the early twentieth century there seems to have been almost as many ghosts as people living in this grand old house. And then another one took up residence in 1923!

This ghost seemed to have been linked to an old bed brought into the house by the new owner, Professor Ian Holbourn. It was a bed once slept in by Charles I, who had his head cut off (although not while in the bed!).

The bed had a habit of unmaking itself, as if someone had slept in it. This was after it had been made by the chambermaid, who would turn round moments later only to see all her work undone. Needless to say, it terrified her!

If someone slept in the bed, strange noises could be heard. Thumps and creaking sounds came from the room even when nobody was in it. Understandably, the servants hated going into the room.

Then, one day in 1925, a special visitor arrived. Her name was Avis Dolphin. Holbourn had invited her because they had both been on the *Titanic* and he had saved her life, and so they had remained in touch. Guess which bedroom she was given. Yes, the one with the haunted bed!

Avis had no idea the house was haunted. She was woken by a noise downstairs. As she went down to investigate, Professor Holbourn heard noises in the bedroom.

'I told you not to put her in that room,' his wife said. 'Go and see she's alright.' And so the professor put on his gown and walked along the corridor and stood listening outside the bedroom door. There was the sound of walking, then a crash, so he opened the door. The bedroom was empty. Just at that moment, Avis appeared from downstairs.

'There were noises,' she said, 'strange noises downstairs.'

'Never mind,' said the professor, not wanting to tell her too much in case she got afraid. 'Tomorrow we will give you a quieter room.'

Avis was tired so she went back to bed. She soon fell asleep. There was no other incident that night.

The following evening, she was getting ready to go to bed. As she was unfurling her hair she felt the air go cold, and then she screamed. The professor and his wife came running.

'Something touched me,' she said, 'as if someone had run their fingertip across my neck!'

This wasn't the last time a ghost was seen or felt in the house, but it is said that these days the hauntings have now stopped. Perhaps the ghosts have moved.

Maybe to your house!

23

THE GHOST OF INNERWICK

The Reverend William Ogilvie was minister for Innerwick in the early eighteenth century. On the evening of 3 February 1722, he was riding back home in the dark along the burial road from Thurston, when he heard a horse ride up behind him.

'Who's there?' cried Ogilvie into the darkness. A shadowy figure approached and replied, 'I am the Laird of Cool.'

Ogilvie knew this couldn't be true, for the Laird of Cool had recently passed away. It must be someone trying to play a practical joke, he thought. And so to teach the joker a lesson, Ogilvie slowed his horse, and when the figure approached he swung his cane to hit him as hard as he could. But the cane just whizzed through the figure, as if there was nothing there! The minister was almost unseated and lost his grip on the cane, which flew onto the ground.

The shadowy stranger laughed as the now ruffled minister got off his horse and searched for the cane. He found it but by now his body was trembling, partly with fear and partly with anger. He struggled back onto his horse, and continued to ride home, now in very anxious state. But the stranger continued to follow him, so once again the minister demanded the stranger identify himself.

'I telt ye, I am the Laird of Cool,' replied the stranger. The minister stared at the shadowy figure. The light was not good, and the minister now found himself doubting what he saw. It seemed like a spectre, indeed, it seemed to be a ghost. Terror gripped his throat, but then he gathered his courage and asked him: 'Well if you are who you say you are, what do you want with me?'

The ghost replied that he had heard of one of the minister's sermons and believed he was a good man. He would like to ask him to pass on some information to his grieving and loving wife. Taken aback, the minster asked the ghost how he knew about the sermon, wondering if he had been there but invisible. 'You maun ken that we are acquainted wi mony things that the living ken nathing aboot,' was the ghost's reply.

When they reached the churchyard at Innerwick, the ghost bade Ogilvie farewell, with the words: 'I see ye are in some disorder, I will return when ye hae mair presence of mind.' The ghost then vanished with an awful singing and buzzing noise, which finally terrified the poor minister.

'Whit's wrang wi ye?' asked the minister's wife when he arrived home. 'It looks like ye've seen a ghost! Ye ailing frae something ma dear?'

Ogilvie just shook his head. 'It's cauld oot,' he said, 'I may hae a fever.'

'I'll get ye a dram,' his wife said, 'a guid nicht's sleep is whit ye need.'

He went to bed early after his dram, but he couldn't sleep. How could he? It's not every day a ghost chums you home, and he was still trembling from the experience.

In the morning, it all seemed like a bad dream and the minister half forgot his strange encounter. Not long after, on 5 March, he was called to Harehead to baptise a shepherd's child. On his return to Innerwick, the ghost once again appeared.

'Dinnae be feart,' said the ghost. But the minister was ready this time. He was a man of faith, and knew God would protect him, and so had no fear. In fact, he had been looking forward to this promised meeting, for he had prepared a number of questions to ask the ghost, 'concerning the affairs of the other world'.

The ghost agreed to answer the questions if the minister would then agree to help him in return, by passing a message to his wife. The minister agreed to think about it.

And so the ghost was interrogated by the minister with a series of questions. The minister discovered that the ghost could travel from one place to another in a blink of an eye, that his body was not his own, and that the horse he was riding on was in fact Andrew Johnson, who had once been a tenant of his!

The minister also asked what heaven and hell were like. Those in heaven, said the ghost, had the 'serenity of their minds', while those in hell suffered from the 'stings of an awakened conscience'.

The discussion ended as they arrived at Innerwick, but the minister was well satisfied with the answers to his questions and so was happy to meet again, which they did a month later on 5 April, as he was returning from Oldhamstocks. This time it was the ghost's turn to ask his favour.

The ghost seemed to have the need to confess the sins of his earthly life. 'During ma mortal life, I wis a cheat and liar. I maun say I swindled mony gentle folk frae their siller unjustly.' He had, he said, also gained a fortune by forging documents, and in so doing had ruined many people's lives. The ghost listed those who had fallen victim to his fraud and corruption, one of whom was the minister's own father-in-law.

'Please, I beg ye, gang tae ma gudewife and tell her a this,' asked the ghost, 'she has sufficient funds tae repay a that which I took unjustly.'

'But surely if ye tell her yersel she will mair readily listen, sae why won't you tell her?' enquired the minister.

'Because I will not,' replied the ghost.

The minister asked for a reason, but the ghost refused to explain. 'However, if you do as I ask I will explain everything,' he pleaded. The minister could see the ghost was desperate to rid himself of the burning guilt he felt and make amends for the wrong he had done.

'I will hae tae think aboot this,' said Ogilvie, as they once again arrived at the walls of Innerwick churchyard.

The final meeting took place five days later, at Pees, as the minister was coming back from Old Camus. By this time he had made up his mind.

'If I gang tae see yer gudewife, why would she believe me? How can I prove a this? I will mak a fool o' maself. Folk will think I am brain sick or mad! Please do not insist on this. Let's leave this request till oor next meeting.'

'Very weel,' agreed the ghost reluctantly.

But there was no next meeting, as the Reverend Ogilvie died soon afterwards.

Soon after the minster's death, documents were discovered in his desk. They were clearly meant to have been secret, as they were in a locked drawer. These documents gave an account of the minister's meetings with the ghost, and their discussions, which is why we know about them. They became a bestselling chapbook!

Ghostly apparitions are still seen on dark nights at Innerwick. Perhaps it is the ghost of the Laird of Cool who still wanders with his guilty conscience.

24

TALLY SINCLAIR

George is Haddington born and bred, and he began work as an apprentice printer for the *East Lothian Courier* at the age of 15, in 1961. The building he worked in is located on a corner in Market Street, which was then the *East Lothian Courier* offices.

The day he began his apprenticeship, he walked into the old building and was immediately struck by its ancient feel. The floorboards creaked, the old walls seemed to drip history, and the print room in the basement had a 'Dickensian atmosphere'.

George had only been working there a day or two when he was told by workmates of a ghost that inhabited the building.

'I's the ghost of Tally Sinclair,' George was told.

'Who was that?' asked George, not really believing in ghosts.

His workmate explained, 'He was a candlemaker in the previous century. Everybody knows he walks about the house.'

George shrugged his shoulders. He didn't believe in ghosts.

But then, one night, George was in the basement all by himself, working the guillotine. As usual he was wearing a long blue overall. Suddenly, someone behind him tugged his overall twice. He quickly turned round, expecting to see a colleague, but there was nobody there! George was spooked, and despite the fact that he hadn't believed in ghosts, in that moment he was convinced that the ghost of Tally Sinclair was in the room with him.

He studied the room carefully, peering into its dark corners, but could see nothing. He still had his job to finish so he couldn't leave. He continued to work, but now his ears were on red alert. Every wee noise, every creak had him staring into the shadows. When

he finally finished his job, he couldn't get out of the basement fast enough.

This was the only time George had a personal encounter with Tally Sinclair, but other workmates had similar experiences. He worked with the *East Lothian Courier* for forty-three years and witnessed many changes, but not as many as Tally Sinclair!

The *Courier* is no longer produced from the building with Tally's ghost and these days another organisation occupies the premises.

'They don't need to worry,' said George with a smile, 'if it is Tally then he is obviously a friendly ghost, I think he just wants to say hello every now and then. Folk quite often stop at the corner outside the basement window to have a blether. I'm sure Tally enjoys listening to all the town gossip!'

25

THE HAUNTED WELL OF AMISFIELD

This tale was shared by Andrew Stoddart, an East Lothian farmer.

John Thomson was a farm servant from Middle Hailes in East Lothian. On the first Friday of February, 1888, he made his way to Haddington for an annual event called 'Hiring Friday'. This was when farmers hired servants for the following year, and so it was a major occasion in the work calendar of the county. Many farm hands would converge on the town, looking for work. But of course, it was also a major social occasion.

John spent longer than planned in the town, as he had met some friends he hadn't seen in a while. They drank together and had a very convivial evening, so convivial in fact that they didn't notice the deteriorating weather outside.

It had been a cold and harsh winter, and the landscape this February was still strewn with snow. An icy wind had picked up as the evening turned into night and the snell wind nipped John's face the moment he left the tavern. Maybe he should have tried to find a place to stay in Haddington, but he had no money, and anyway it wasn't such a long walk, and his merry state would help make his journey feel swifter.

He accompanied his friends across Nungate Bridge over the Tyne and then parted with them at the West Lodge Gate of Amisfield. He had decided to take a shortcut through the policies

of Amisfield, known as Amisfield Park, where Haddington Golf
Course was established in 1865.

One of his friends looked at him, horrified. 'Ye maun be careful,'
said his friend, 'it's near midnicht sae tak care as ye go near the
haunted well!'

John wasn't worried. He called back to his friend, 'Och, I dinnae
belive in that kind o' speerits!' he said jokingly.

He then made his way along the drive. He walked quickly, his
pace aided by his light head.

The snow was crisp here, and in the still and cold night the crunching sound of his footsteps seemed almost to echo into the night. Although dark, the snow illuminated his way and soon he veered off the main drive and headed directly home, taking him through an area known as 'the Jungle' because of the trees and thick undergrowth there.

Then he heard the Haddington Town clock strike midnight. He stopped walking and stood motionless. Something had caught his attention. It was a sound. He stood listening and realised it was the wind which had suddenly picked up. It was brushing the leafless branches of the trees, making an eerie noise.

He now felt horribly sober. He continued his journey but the trees were taking on weird shapes in the darkness. A branch seemed to grab him, and the fright it gave him sent a shudder down his spine. It started to snow, and the journey now seemed longer than anticipated.

Then John realised he was approaching the haunted well. Now he felt uneasy. He tried to reason with himself, but a rising sense of fear was taking over his senses. His heart raced. He was not alone in the darkness.

There was a figure, slowly moving towards the well. It had its head bowed down as if there was something wrong with the neck, and it was wringing its hands. It seemed in deep agony and despair. John watched as it glided towards the well and then, unbelievably, disappeared into it.

John's body initially froze with terror. But then his legs were electrified and he ran, ran faster than he had ever done in his life, and didn't stop until he reached Middle Hailes. He was in a state of complete exhaustion and terror when he arrived home, and he was only later able to tell his story.

The well is supposed to be located in the policies of Amisfield House, which was built in 1755 but demolished in the 1920s. The clubhouse of Haddington Golf Course now stands on the site.

But an earlier house also once stood here, called Newmills. This was the home of Sir James Stanfield, who was murdered. His son Philip was convicted of the crime. Is it his ghost that was seen?

He was refused a burial after his execution, and his corpse was hung up for display there (although his right hand was nailed to Haddington's East Gate). But his body was stolen twice. After the first disappearance, it was found lying in water. But when it was stolen the second time, it was never recovered.

The ghost is wringing his hands in despair, head bent over as if there is something wrong with the neck. Philip's end was gruesome. The hanging was botched and so he had to be strangled by the executioner, just as he'd done to his father.

Is the ghost perhaps not wringing his hands, but clenching his remaining one over the right arm? His head bowed because of the manner of his death? And wailing because he remains undiscovered, and perhaps a victim of injustice? We must remember he had always protested his innocence. Maybe he was innocent, as many have since argued. The main evidence against him was that his father's body bled when he touched it.

Is there something within that ancient well, some gruesome hidden secret, waiting to be discovered?

26

ISABEL HERIOT OF PEASTON

Peaston is an ancient village in a quiet corner in the south-west of the county. Its old, dilapidated pantiled houses create a picturesque picture of times gone by. It was here, in the late 1670s, that an old woman called Isabel Heriot worked as a servant for the minister.

If truth be told, Isabel hadn't been blessed with the best of looks. Her neck was also very slightly crooked, which made her gait look strange, and she walked in an unusual manner as a result. She was unusually small in stature and her dark complexion led many local gossips to conclude she was a gypsy.

When she came into the employment of the minister, nobody was sure of her origins. She had no family in the area, and no relatives ever came visiting. She had little time for socialising anyway as she worked very hard. From the moment she got up until her bedtime, she was busy keeping house and attending to the minister's needs. No one, the minister included, could fault Isabel on her work.

This kept her safe from the malicious gossip about who she was and where she came from. It was a dangerous time to be different, especially if you were a poor old woman with no family to help and defend you, for such people were particularly vulnerable to charges of witchcraft, just by nature of their difference.

Yet after some time, despite her hard work and devotion to her duty, she fell foul of the minister's displeasure. The minister was a stern and hellfire type, very common in those days, and although Isabel faithfully attended kirk every Sunday, the minister believed she did not take the service seriously enough.

He noticed on more than one occasion that she was talking while in the middle of preaching. Even worse, during one of his sermons Isabel even fell asleep, which of course enraged the self-righteous minister. How could she talk or sleep while the words of God were being spoken!

But there was something else about Isabel that annoyed the minister even more. She was a very confident and articulate speaker, and had none of the submissive shyness expected of someone of her lowly station. Instead of 'knowing her place', she spoke to people of high rank as if they were her equals. And horror of horrors, she could ride a horse as well as any nobleman, and took any opportunity to show off her riding skills!

In addition to this, she had a sharp and mischievous sense of humour, with a loud laugh that came from her belly. When she mingled with members of the congregation after service, there were often waves of laughter and jocularity, as Isabel took the rare opportunity to mix socially. Needless to say, her jokes and sense of fun were not appreciated by the minister. And so, one day, he summoned her to his room.

'Isabel, why dae ye sleep when the word o' God is being spoken?' he asked her.

'Forgie me sir,' she replied, 'I wis sae tired frae my early morning work cleaning the ashes, I closed my een, but I wasnae asleep, I did hear your words.' She then went on to recite some of the scripture he had used in the sermon to prove she had been attentive.

'And why dae ye speak tae yer superiors as if ye were equal tae them, and ride a horse as if ye were a man?' he chided her.

'Sir, are we not a' servants o' God, and equal in his een?' she replied.

The minister lost his temper, 'Enough o' this impudence! I am done wi ye. You maun leave at once.'

'But sir,' she begged, 'I have nae place tae go. I hae worked here maist ma life, devoted masel tae serving you, and those before ye. Please dinnae cast me oot.'

But the minister was unmoved and determined to sack her.

When Isabel realised the minister was deadly serious, she could hardly believe it. How could he be so cruel and thankless? She had worked her fingers to the bone for him. Everyone knew how hard she worked. Even the minister had to admit her work had been faultless. The job had been her life, but this all counted for nothing. He was offended by her intelligence and confidence.

And so she lost not only her livelihood but her home as well, for she was turned out of the house. Even until the last moment she hoped that somewhere in that man's heart of cold, self-righteous

stone there would be a flicker of humanity and concern for her. But no, he turned his back on her and forced her to leave.

As she left, her sadness turned to anger. She picked up a stone and hurled it at the front door. It hit the door with a loud bang. The minister ignored it. Isabel stood for a moment, utterly devastated, with no idea where to go. Nobody in the area offered to help, and she knew she dare not ask, for the minister's power over the local folk meant she was now very vulnerable. And so she left the village, with just a sack of meagre belongings.

She lived with the rabbits in a local wood, but it was 1680 and when the winter arrived it was severe and long. Isabel didn't survive it.

A few days after she passed away, the minister was in his house when some stones were thrown at his front door. He looked out the window, and just glimpsed a figure in white clothes vanish into the night darkness. Some days later, the minister came down to his stable one morning to get his horse and he noticed it was sweating. It had obviously been ridden, but by whom?

Other strange things happened. The minister's nightcap was taken from his head while sleeping, and he found it full of ashes! Soon people began to see the strange figure in white clothes. It was a woman, and she looked just like Isabel Heriot!

The strange happenings and sightings continued for a while, but then ceased. Perhaps poor Isabel had moved to a better place and was finally able to rest in peace.

27

THE GREEN LADY OF MARKET STREET

Musselburgh is perhaps the oldest town in Scotland. We can trace its origins as far back as the Romans, and the River Esk has undoubtedly made it an attractive place to settle ever since humans first arrived in the area.

The old bridge, or Roman Bridge as it is traditionally called, is one of the wonders of East Lothian. It reeks of antiquity and was once the main crossing over the Esk. As such, the footprints of Scotland's history are imbedded in its ancient stones.

While original Roman masonry may still be encased within its arches, what we see today is the result of later medieval repairs and rebuilding. It is, just like Musselburgh town itself, a mixture of ages with antiquity at its core.

And Market Street that leads to it is likewise a route of great antiquity, although much has changed here. 'Progress' and development has robbed the street of much of its historic character, although, like the bridge at its end, the parade of key moments in Scotland's history has literally marched this way.

A house called Eden Cottage once stood in this street. It was a picturesque eighteenth-century structure, surrounded by a high boundary wall. Some Musselburgh residents may still remember it, and if so they may also remember the legend of the Green Lady associated with it.

There are many Green Lady ghost tales in East Lothian, but the Green Lady who haunted Eden Cottage no longer has her home, and so she now walks up and down Market Street, and can be seen wandering close by her old house, which is now occupied by more modern housing.

Tradition has not passed down her name, but she was a very beautiful young woman when she lived in the cottage in the eighteenth century. She lived alone as a single independent woman, at a time when women were subject to the control of male family members.

She had two suitors who competed with each other to win her affections, but she could not decide which one to choose. The details of this threesome we don't know, but as we do know, threesomes rarely have a happy ending.

Unable to make up her mind, the two men decided to settle the matter with a sword duel. When she discovered that the two men she cared for most were going to fight over her in such a foolish manner, she resolved to prevent it.

She had made up her mind who she truly loved, and so now there was no need for them to settle the matter in such a brutal manner. She would declare her fondness for them both, but her love for only one. She now knew what her heart felt.

She rushed to the scene of the duel with a sense of rising panic, and when she arrived her fears were confirmed: she was too late. One of her suitors lay dead on the bloodstained grass. She ran towards the body, unaware of the presence of the victor. Her footsteps slowed as she approached the dead man.

'Oh no,' she tried to say, but the words were soundless. She fell to her knees and sobbed over the body of the man she now knew she had truly loved.

The other man tried to console her, but how could he? In his own desire to be with her he had killed the man she had really loved. How could she possibly be with him?

In her grief, she fled back to her cottage. An apple tree with strong branches grew outside her window. The following day she was found. In her grief, she had hanged herself from the tree.

But, according to the legend, her ghost was soon to be seen in the house where she once lived. And the haunting continued well into the twentieth century.

One tenant in the late 1920s reported waking one night. She happened to glance towards the window and saw a spectre of a woman standing in front of the window. Fright electrified her body and she put on the light, which caused the spectre to vanish.

Later, her husband William, who was a dentist, was relaxing in the lounge when their two dogs began a frenzy of barking. When William opened the door to see what was disturbing the animals,

he witnessed the outline of a woman descending the stairs towards him. He stood aghast as the woman elegantly but sadly floated downwards, stared at him and then just vanished in a shaft of light.

Other tenants also reported sightings of the Green Lady, although strangely they all described her as grey, rather than green. On one occasion, a tenant was awoken in the dead of night and when he opened his eyes the woman was standing over him, only to quickly vanish.

But then, just over sixty years ago, the cottage was demolished to make way for a development of thirty-two new houses. So the homeless ghost became the 'Green Lady of Market Street'.

She is said to wander up and down the street, quietly but sadly. She seems to have a habit of looming up to men, staring at them and then vanishing. Perhaps she is looking for the man she once loved in life, but left it too late to tell him her true feelings.

28

THE HOLY ROOD WELL

Stenton is a charming old village. The red pantiled houses are a delight on a sunny day, settled as they are in picturesque East Lothian countryside. One of the features of the village is an old tron, a weighing machine used to measure the weight of goods bought and sold in the village market in days gone by.

Close by, on the edge of the village, there is the sixteenth-century Well of the Holy Rood. Its beautifully made conical stone roof makes it look like a wee house. It is made of dressed and smoothed stone, and on the top there is a flowered finial which is said to resemble a cardinal's hat. It is actually older than the rest of the well, and was originally part of the old kirk nearby. It seems this was not just added for decoration, as there is a legend attached to this 'hat'. The legend states that the tenure of Beil Estate depends on the well keeping its hat on! Maybe this is why the structure has been so well preserved.

It was obviously once an important place of local pilgrimage, as there used to be a stone path leading to it from the church. But our story took place in the early nineteenth century, when this ancient well was a scene of a near-tragic comical drama.

It was a very hot day and a thirsty cow grazing in a nearby field wandered to the well. It stuck its head into the opening of the well, in an attempt to drink the water to relieve its thirst. However, the water was way too deep down to reach.

But the cow didn't give up and squeezed itself further into the well, stretching its neck and sticking out its tongue. Still the water was too far away. But the smell of the water was so tempting and the cow so thirsty that it squeezed its body and reached down as far as it could.

Workers in the nearby field saw the amusing sight of a cow's behind sticking out of the well entrance. But their laughter stopped when the front part of the cow slipped out of sight, lifting its hind legs off the ground as the animal slid down into the well. The cow was now in a very precarious position, and mooing loudly in distress from within the well.

The farm hands ran to the well and attempted to pull the poor creature from its predicament. It would still have been funny, if the cow wasn't now clearly terrified and in pain.

And so began a rescue operation. Boys were sent for more help from the village, and a crowd assembled around the poor animal's backside, as they discussed the best way to rescue the cow from the well.

It was a valuable animal, so great care had to be taken as they slowly and carefully raised the traumatised cow, backside first, out of the well. The cow then walked back to the field seemingly unhurt, to the cheers of the villagers. It was not long after this incident that the decision was made to fill in the well.

It now sits quietly by the road just outside the village as you travel towards Dunbar, a monument to past beliefs. A metal grille gate guards the entrance!

It really is an unusual and beautifully made structure, and worth a visit if you are passing through this beautiful village.

29

THE HOLY WELL AND THE MYSTERY OF DUNBAR'S LOST HEROINE

Our Lady's Well at Whitekirk is a place once considered so sacred that it was a site of pilgrimage for many years. A shrine was erected with a statue of Mary, which was visited by thousands of people in medieval times.

There is a document in the Vatican which tells a tale of how this well became so important. The writer is anonymous and it was written after the Reformation. The story takes us to the 1290s, when Scotland was invaded by the English King Edward I.

These were horrible times. Edward was a ruthless king and his attempted conquest of Scotland brought misery and death to so many. It also brought division, as many Scottish nobles also had English lands and so felt their interests lay with Edward I.

The story in the Vatican document tells us that Agnes, Countess of Dunbar, having held the castle against Edward's forces, fled from the castle rather than be captured. The author wrote that, 'Black Agness countess of Dunbar … rather than fall into the hands of her enemies, made her escape by water.'

She hoped to flee to Fife, but the prevailing wind sent her to the coast closest to Fairknowe. She had been injured in her escape. The document doesn't tell us how, but says she was in great pain. She would have had to scramble in haste onto the boat, down rocks, in the dark. No wonder she was injured.

But landing on the shore was not the end of the danger. English patrols were everywhere, the Scots had been routed in battle. With a few followers she hid in woods and hollows, but remained in great pain.

The writer tells us she prayed to the Holy Mother and as she did so, a hermit heard her words.

'Drink of that well, which is sacred, and if you have faith, then you will find relief from your bodily pain,' he told her.

She did so, and as she drank, her bruises and injuries miraculously healed. In gratitude, she endowed a chapel and chantry. Word of the miraculous powers of the waters soon spread. People began to visit the well, and it became a place of great pilgrimage.

Later, in 1355, a party of English sailors arrived at the shrine, and one of the sailors saw a ring on the finger of the statue of Mary. He pulled at it but it wouldn't come off. So he took hold of the image and grabbed at the ring with all his might. The sailor broke the finger from the hand and slid off the ring. He had little time to admire the object of his theft, as a crucifix fell on his head 'and dashed his brains out'.

And there was more vengeance to come. The sailors took away sacred and valuable objects from this shrine, as well as others; but they never reached home. A great storm whipped up giant waves, and the sailors and their ill-gotten gains were sent to the bottom of the sea just off Tynemouth. And there they remain.

But the well and chapel continued to be a place of great pilgrimage, with thousands of people visiting every year. It was re-named White Chapel, or Whitekirk, in 1430.

The author of the Vatican document wrote of these events in the years after the Scottish Reformation. He was lamenting the decline of the well's importance, saying pilgrims were no longer safe, that the shrine had been smashed and any offerings were being taken. The new Protestant religion, of course, had no place for such holy shrines.

And so the well was lost and a place once so important was almost forgotten. But clues to its location suggest a marshy pool nearby the kirk is in fact the site of the well.

But there is something else significant about the story of the origins of Our Lady's Well. The author was writing of events which had taken place about 270 years before, and it seems clear he got the dates wrong. He said that, 'in 1294 when Edward First of England had defeated the Scots army at Dunbar, many of the army fled into the castle'. The date was not 1294, but 1296. It's a simple mistake to make considering he was writing of events so long ago; but then again, maybe he did write 1296, as a 6 could be mistaken for a 4 if the quill pen slipped or dripped.

And there is another crucial mistake. He says, 'Black Agnes, Countess of Dunbar, who, seeing the number within so great that the place must soon be surrendered, rather than fall into the hands of her enemies, made her escape.'

Indeed, we know that after the disastrous battle of Dunbar in 1296, many of the Scots were given refuge in Dunbar Castle, so he has got that right. But the story of Black Agnes's escape? This is a clear mistake. For sure, Black Agnes is famous for her defiance of the English who were besieging Dunbar Castle, but that was in 1338, not 1296! Black Agnes wasn't even born in 1296!

This is not a simple a mistake, it is a major inaccuracy which undermines the whole story of the foundation of the holy well. It would mean the shrine was founded by a woman who escaped from Dunbar Castle, who had not even been born!

How could he make such a blunder? The answer is, very easily. And his mistake might unlock a mystery about Dunbar's lost heroine.

Marjorie Comyn was the grandmother of Black Agnes. And wait for this: she also bravely held Dunbar Castle against the English, in 1296! How could the author confuse their identity? Well, both their husbands had similar names and both were Earls of Dunbar. So both women had the same title, Duchess of Dunbar, and of course, they both defiantly held the castle against besieging English forces!

So the author of the Vatican document got confused between these two Countesses of Dunbar. It's understandable, given they were related and their stories are so similar, and that they both bravely and defiantly held Dunbar Castle during the Wars of Independence.

But there is also a good reason why the writer made this mistake. The actions of Black Agnes, Countess of Dunbar, became legendary. Her story has been celebrated and told down the ages. Yet her heroic grandmother just vanished from history, there is no account of what happened to her, no legendary tales, she just goes missing and is almost unknown. So it's no wonder the writer confused them and assumed it was the famous granddaughter who was the countess who founded the well.

But the story of the founding of Our Lady's Well fits perfectly for Marjorie, Countess of Dunbar. And it partly unlocks the mystery of what may have happened to her.

Marjorie's husband, Cospatrick, Earl of Dunbar, had sided with Edward I in 1296. He set off from Dunbar Castle to join forces with the English army, and left Marjorie in charge, with orders to hold the castle against the Scots! She gave no indication that she would disobey her husband, but the moment he was out of sight, she made it clear she was holding the castle for the Scots! She was, after all, a Comyn, and both her father and brother were in the Scottish army that assembled at Dunbar in 1296.

The battle that then ensued nearby was a terrible disaster for the Scots, and remnants of the Scots army fled to Dunbar. Marjorie opened the castle's gates for them and gave them refuge. When her husband arrived with the English king, she defied them.

You can imagine the scene. Her husband embarrassed and enraged, the English king determined to teach the defiant Scots inside a lesson. So Edward I ordered the castle to be taken, and we know at this point Marjorie was alive and in the castle. But what happens next is chilling. She just vanishes. There is no record of what happened to her.

Edward I was a brutal man. Only weeks before, he had ordered the massacre of innocents at Berwick upon Tweed (then a Scottish town) because of their defiance. Marjorie could expect no mercy from him. And she'd humiliated her husband, so he was unlikely to defend her. Her end could have been extremely unpleasant. Most have assumed she was killed and quietly disposed of, along with the memory of her heroic defiance.

But does the tale of Our Lady's Well give us a clue that she did in fact escape? The story fits. But what happened to her after she hid in the hollow, and drank from the well? Was she captured? Or did she get away, maybe even join Wallace in the woods not so far away?

Edward liked to make examples of people who defied him. If Marjorie had been captured, either in the castle or afterwards, then surely she would have been publicly humiliated. The fact there is no mention of her adds to the idea she escaped. This was further defiance, and not something Edward or Marjorie's husband would want advertised.

So maybe the silence about her heroism is rooted in her secret escape. As a fugitive, she perhaps didn't want to court too much publicity. It seems the truth remains elusive and still a mystery.

Yet whatever the truth of it, Marjorie Comyn deserves recognition as a brave and defiant patriot and a woman of independent will.

30

THE WARRIOR NUN

Not far from the Abbey Bridge by Haddington, there grows an ancient sycamore tree. Its bark is twisted and crinkled with age, and its deep-set trunk supports old branches that fan upwards like ageing arms. Its roots are entwined round dressed stones which once clearly formed part of a man-made structure. Perhaps this was part of the channel that led water to the now derelict nearby mill. But perhaps, also, these stones were once part of the abbey which used to stand proudly on this very spot.

It's almost impossible to believe that an abbey once stood on the banks of the river, on this now tranquil and beautiful spot. But the name Abbey Bridge gives away the fact that this was once the site of a thriving religious community.

It had ancient origins, for it was founded in the twelfth century by a Northumbrian countess who became a princess in Scotland.

Her name was Ada de Warenne. She became the wife of Prince Henry, who was the son of David I of Scotland. The lands around Hadddington were granted to her as part of her marriage settlement.

We get mere glimpses of her from history. She lived in Haddington, which in those days was one of the major market towns of the kingdom. She had seven children, two of them became kings of Scotland. Ada was deeply religious and committed to promoting the church, just as her father-in-law's mother had been.

And so, in 1178, towards the end of her life, she founded a Cistercian abbey just east of where the Abbey Bridge now stands. It was occupied by an order of nuns and dedicated to the Virgin Mary.

It looked over the Tyne here for around 400 years, yet barely a trace of it is now left. Yet the voice of legend echoes here, and tells us of a great event that took place in the year 1358.

It was 8 September, an important date for the church as it was the feast of the nativity of the Virgin. In essence, it was the Virgin Mary's birthday, and a celebratory feast was taking place inside the abbey.

Prayers were being said, and singing swirled round the columns of the abbey. But outside, the river was swelling and rising. Days of heavy rain had raised the level of the river and now it threatened to breach its banks. Further upstream, villages had been swept away, and the barony of Nungate had been overwhelmed and completely destroyed.

Evidence of the devastation upstream could now be seen in the murky and rising waters. The noise of rushing water made the nuns cease their devotions and venture outside to assess the danger. As they looked upstream, they saw a raging torrent approaching. The water was full of debris, scraping along the banks. When it arrived at the curve where the abbey stood, the nuns were forced to retreat. The river no longer had banks, it was a violent swathe of water sweeping all before it like an angry, vengeful hand. Trees were being uprooted as the banks collapsed. It was an inland tsunami, and the abbey was in its path.

The nuns, who had been praying, took flight from this flood of biblical proportions. Except one; she ran into the Lady Chapel. But she did not fall to her knees and pray this time. Instead, she climbed up onto the altar and wrapped her arms around the statue of the Virgin Mary. She lifted it from the plinth and carried it out of the abbey and then to the edge of the raging waters outside.

She stood with a rage of her own. With all her strength, she raised the statue of the Virgin above her head. The water began to swirl around her ankles and she could see a wave approaching her.

'Sister!' cried one of her fellow nuns. 'Sister, you will be swept away, all is lost, come save yourself!'

But the nun had the courage of a warrior and she stood firm in her faith and determination.

'I defy you in the name of her Lady,' she cried out. 'I call on the Virgin Mother, lay your hands upon this vengeful tide, I beseech you, make it subside!'

But the wall of water approached with undying speed.

'Sister, in the name of mercy, come away,' cried the fellow nun who was now running for her life.

The abbey seemed doomed. But the warrior nun stood defiantly.

'Virgin Mary,' she cried out, 'the abbey and my life is dedicated to you. I call on you to save us!' She paused, then took in a deep breath so she could yell at the top of her voice, and what she said next was shocking!

She cried out: 'Otherwise I will cast your sacred image into the water where it will perish!'

This was blackmail! Blackmailing the mother of God was not part of church teaching!

But suddenly, the wall of water miraculously lost its force and dissipated. It slapped harmlessly on the abbey's walls and soon the flood began to withdraw, harmlessly sweeping over the feet of the warrior nun who still stood, holding the Virgin Mary to the heavens.

The abbey was saved!

The warrior nun wept and gave thanks, while her sisters fell to their knees proclaiming a miracle. She carefully lowered the statue and walked back into the abbey. She put the statue back onto its plinth, and now she too fell to her knees in humble submission and thanks.

The warrior nun's bravery, and the divine intervention it enlisted, made the abbey all the more famous, but she remained an unnamed legend, and so because of her bravery and courage I have named her the warrior nun.

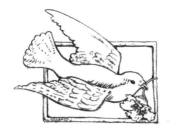

31

A LEGEND OF FEARFUL CHARACTER

Danskein Inn was in many ways like an oasis on the edge of a desert. It stood on the edge of the Lammermuir Hills, just south of Gifford, where the road south climbs into wild and rugged moorland. Travellers would stop for the night, enjoy the hospitality and set off early the next morning, with the maximum of daylight hours available for travel.

On one occasion, a mounted traveller unusually arrived in early morning seeking some breakfast and time to rest before heading further south. The innkeeper had an instinct for people, and his instinct was telling him that this stranger was suspicious. But at the same time, business is business, and so the traveller was welcomed at this unusual hour and his needs met.

The innkeeper was determined to find out more. He was very good at small talk and lacing casual conversation with probing questions about his guests' lives. But as he served this customer, all his usual lines of enquiry were met by a reluctance to give any information at all.

Who was this mysterious traveller? And where had he spent the night, given that he arrived at the inn just as morning was breaking? Did he live nearby? What was the purpose of his journey? What was his business? What was his name? The innkeeper could find out nothing. The traveller answered the landlord's questions without really answering:

'Och, nearby. Tae get tae where I'm going. Tae find oot the truth o' the matter. Ma name is o' nae consequence.' How frustrating it was for the innkeeper. And so eventually he gave up and the guest was left to eat in solitude.

After a hearty breakfast, the traveller called for his bill. The landlord watched as the mysterious guest delved into his pocket and took out a very full-looking purse. He fumbled with it, searching for the correct coins. It looked like he was travelling with a small fortune.

This just made the landlord all the more curious. Who would travel with such a heavy purse? Perhaps this mysterious man was a robber? He was dressed roughly, without style, yet he had a small fortune on him. His horse was of good quality yet his clothes were simple. It didn't add up.

'Ye maun tak care oot oan the hills,' said the innkeeper as his guest prepared himself to leave. 'The weather is nae friend tae man or beast at this time o' year, and folk roond here ken that a wolf stalks the way tae Duns.'

'A wolf?' asked the traveller, suddenly taking interest in what the landlord was saying.

'Och aye,' said the innkeeper, 'folk say it's a white wolf. It stalks the road at this time o' year an mony a traveller has vanished as a result.'

The traveller nodded his head in recognition. 'Aye, I have heard something o' that. People have vanished oan the moor, but I ay thocht the tale o' the wolf wis just auld wimmin's talk. Are no a' the wolves now gone?'

'Auld wimmin hae mair sense than we ken,' replied the innkeeper. Then he added, 'I am quiet this time o' year, and have a room for ye if ye decide ye dinnae want tae venture ony further.'

It wasn't an offer made out of kindness or hospitality, of course, but business. This man had money, lots of it.

But the traveller was determined to be on his way. He thanked the landlord for his service and mounted his horse. The innkeeper watched as the mysterious traveller merged into the moorland, mounted on his horse.

It was a day on the fringe of winter. The low-lying sun was streaming across the moorland, but it didn't have the power to lift the cold hanging mist that clung onto the heather. It was eerily quiet, and the main sound the traveller could hear was that of his horse snorting and breathing as it climbed steeply further into the hills.

Then suddenly another sound filled the air. The traveller pulled his horse to, and scoured the moor with his eyes. The sound was unmistakable. It was a horse galloping at full speed. It was coming from behind him, and when he turned round he saw a man on a horse approaching rapidly.

It was the Danskein innkeeper! As he approached the traveller, he could make out that the landlord had a pistol in his right hand.

Frozen onto his saddle, the traveller watched as the landlord raised his hand and fired the pistol.

The shot whizzed past the traveller harmlessly, but the innkeeper began to reload. The traveller lost no time. He reached into his saddlebag and brought out a bugle. He put it to his lips and blew as hard as he could. The innkeeper was startled at first, then burst into laughter.

'Ye think the dragoons will help ye? Naebody will hear ye up here, and naebody will find ye either aince I'm done wi ye. Another victim o' the wolf!' he said menacingly.

The innkeeper was a murderer and a robber. What better job to have than to run an inn on the edge of a moor, where travellers would stop for the night? Many never made it for breakfast, others who passed by were likewise confronted on the deserted moor by the innkeeper.

Now this mysterious traveller was going to be his next victim. Or so the landlord thought. For this mysterious traveller was none other than the Marquis of Tweeddale. He lived only a couple of miles from Danskein, but had heard rumours of people going missing after visiting the inn.

Nothing was proved, for the innkeeper took the evidence of his crimes onto the moor, where the peat bog kept the secret. But this was now all the evidence the marquis needed. Men sprang from the heather the moment the bugle was sounded. It was a trap set by the marquis.

The innkeeper, suddenly realising he had been fooled, tried to make his escape. But the marquis had set men in all directions. Shots rang out, the landlord fell from his horse, and was quickly apprehended by the marquis's men.

'I should've kent it, I should've kent it,' said the innkeeper as he struggled.

Justice was swift, and that was the end of the Innkeeper of Danskein.

But how many victims had fallen prey to him? The answer lies on the moor, where unmarked graves still hold their secrets.

32

THE LEGEND OF THE LADY OF GAMELSHEIL

The ruins of Gamelsheil Castle stand like jagged teeth on a wild hillside in the Lammermuirs. Lonely these ruins may be today, but they once formed part of a ring of towers which guarded the pass through this wild part of East Lothian. It was then a major route through the hills, and settlements were more widespread there than now. But at the same time there was also woodland on the lower slopes, where now only heather and moorland exist.

In medieval times, the Lady of Gamelsheil lived here with her husband, the keeper of the castle. She was a bonny woman, full of life and humour. She brought colour and energy to the place, and her husband, perhaps unusually for noble marriages of the time, genuinely and deeply loved her.

A noblewoman's life could be lonely at the best of times, but this was a remote posting for a noble wife. Her husband often had business to attend to and on these days she would do her best to while away her time.

At times, there was the opportunity to meet and entertain passing travellers. She was a good and entertaining host, and such times provided some relief from the solitude of life in the tower.

But one of her great joys was wandering from the castle. Often she would go for a walk on the spur of the moment, when the weather was fine or when birdsong filled the air. It would have been the custom for her to be accompanied, but she liked to go for walks on her own. Perhaps up in the hills the social norms of noble society were easier to forget.

The landscape will have held more interest than the bare moorland of today. Nearby there was a favoured place of hers where she would sit by the trickle of the Whiteadder, amongst trees which rustled in the breeze.

One evening, she decided to go for a fateful walk. It was late spring, that time of extended days when the daylight remains even after the sun has submerged below the horizon. She dallied in the gloaming. Perhaps the evening birdsong kept her, perhaps her thoughts.

Suddenly realising the lateness of the hour, she began to return to the castle. But she was being watched. She froze as she saw

something moving in the undergrowth in front of her. Her eyes strained in the semi-darkness to see what it was.

Then it emerged from the shadows. It was a wolf. The animal stared at her, snarling and showing its teeth.

Screams were heard by nearby peasants, who ran to the lady's aid. When they arrived, the wolf's teeth were around her neck. They yelled and screamed at the animal, and threw stones at it. It took fright and fled.

Yet it was too late for the Lady of Gamelsheil. She lay dead where the wolf had left her, within sight of her castle home. One of the peasants rushed to the castle to break the news.

Her husband raced to the scene, and when he saw his beloved wife lying by the burn he sank to his knees and cradled her in his arms.

He was genuinely heartbroken, and he could not bear that his wife would be taken from his view. So he ordered that she be buried within the castle walls. Here she would be close to him, but she would also be safe, for a great fear at the time was wolves digging up the dead in graveyards. The wolf would not be allowed to return to reclaim her, as the tower guarded her as she lay in her protected resting place.

Her husband, it is said, would look out of the window at his bonny wife's grave, eyes swelling in sorrow.

And there, by the ruins of the castle, she still rests. We can be sure the wolf was hunted and killed in revenge, with no one to tell its story.

33

THE LOVESICK COW

The schoolmaster at Prestonpans in the late 1500s was a man called John Fian, although he was also known as Cunningham. He had become besotted with a local maiden. She had no interest in him at all, yet this didn't dampen his ardour for her.

When he heard that he had a rival suitor, John moved quickly and ruthlessly to eliminate this opposition. You see, according to the accounts of the day, John was a man with a knowledge of witchcraft. He used this to make the competitor mad, to horrible effect.

Yet, of course, this still did not make the young woman any more interested in John. No amount of wooing was working. He just wasn't her type and she just wasn't interested. But it so happened that her younger brother was a pupil of John's, and so the schoolmaster decided to use this connection.

John pulled the young boy aside one day and told him that if he did him a favour, then there would be no more beatings. The young boy, of course, was very keen on this idea and so agreed. The schoolmaster then told him what he must do.

In those days, it was common for families to be all crushed together at night, often the family sharing one bed. The schoolmaster told the boy that he wanted three hairs from his sister and that he should take them from her while she slept, so that she had no knowledge of it.

'Then bring them tae me,' said John.

'What dae ye want wi three hairs maister?' asked the curious boy.

'That needna concern ye,' the schoolmaster replied sternly, 'just dae as I say and there'll be nae mair beatings fir ye this term.'

And so that night the young boy waited for his sister to sleep. It was not hairs on the head that the schoolmaster wanted, so the logistics of secretly plucking them without his sister waking up was rather difficult.

'Whit ye daein? Stop fidgeting, and waking me,' his sister protested.

Inevitably the commotion woke their mother.

'Whit's wrang wi ye bairns? Gang tae sleep, it's the middle o' the nicht.'

'It's him,' protested the sister, pointing to her wee brother, 'he cannae keep still.'

The mother was furious that the household had been woken, and so pulled the boy out of bed to punish him.

'Whit's wrang wi ye?' asked the mother angrily. 'Whit are ye wakin yer sister fir?'

The boy told his mother the truth.

'It's the schoolmaister, Ma. He telt me that he wanted three hairs frae ma sister.'

'Whit fir?'

'He telt me that it wasna ma business, but that if I did it he wud stop beating me.'

The mother knew exactly what was going on. It just so happened that she herself had knowledge of witchcraft, and she knew that once the schoolmaster had possession of the hairs, he could use a spell to make her daughter fall in love with him.

In the morning, the mother went outside to the fields where a cow was grazing in the early sunshine. She stroked the cow and then carefully plucked three hairs from its nether region.

She looked at them with a wry smile. 'Aye, they will teach him a lesson,' she thought to herself with a chuckle.

She gave the three hairs to her son.

'Gie them tae the schoolmaister, an tell him that they are hairs frae yer sister.'

The boy did as he was told. He, of course, knew that they were not his sister's hairs, but he was very keen to avoid beatings.

John Fian was overjoyed when the boy slyly handed over the hairs.

'It wasnae easy sir,' he said, 'but here ye are.'

That evening, John started spell-making. He used the hairs in a love potion, a very strong love potion. Whoever had owned the hairs would fall in deep and passionate love with him.

By the morning the potion had worked its magic. The lovestruck cow was waiting for him. It immediately pounced on him in a fit of uncontrolled bovine lust, and then followed him everywhere he went. Classes were interrupted by the mooings and groanings of the cow as it waited outside, craving the attention of Fian. He could go nowhere without being followed by the lovesick cow.

There was a moment when the poor schoolmaster ran past the mother of the young girl, as the lustful cow trotted behind him, trying to catch up.

'That will teach him,' she thought, 'he should have kent it taks one tae ken one.'

34

THE WILD BOAR OF SALTCOATS

One of East Lothian's less well-known castles is Saltcoats, about a mile south of Gullane, reached by a lane extending from Saltcoats Road.

The castle was built around 1592 for Patrick Livingtoun, who owned land stretching from Gullane to North Berwick, and there is a traditional tale which tells us why the Livingtoun family was granted this land.

In the days when wild boar still roamed in Scotland, there was one such animal with a particularly fearsome reputation. It was called the 'Saltcoats' ravenous boar'.

This great creature terrorised the area, and hunters who searched for it shared tales of its great ferocity and brute strength.

One day, an unfortunate lady was suddenly confronted with this notorious creature as she was riding close to the Peffer Burn. The boar was fleeing from hunters and was in a state of high anxiety, and so very dangerous.

Her horse froze as it came face to face with the boar. The woman was seized with fear as the wild pig snorted and drooled, stamped the ground and then charged, ripping into the side of her horse. She fell from her saddle and lay helpless on the ground as the boar then turned and charged once again, this time directly at her.

In that moment, she knew she was going to be gouged by the frightened animal, and closed her eyes with a prayer.

Then, as if by magic, a young man, armed with shield and sword, leapt from the undergrowth. He rushed forward and stood between her and the charging beast. Her clothes had been ripped in her fall so he threw his scarlet cloak over her. Then he faced the boar head on!

The boar charged him, but the young man stood firm and waited until the last moment to act. He rammed his spear into the animal's ribs, but it turned and twisted, snapping the spear. Then the powerful beast tried to use its tusks to gorge at the young man's legs.

But the fearless young man thrust his hand down the throat of the boar, plunging it so deep his entire arm vanished into the great creature. He wore a special glove, which was as long as his arm, and padded with feathers. As the boar choked and spluttered on his arm he wielded his sword, plunging it deep into the animal's breast.

The boar twitched for a few moments, and then the poor defeated animal lay dead. The man then carefully withdrew his arm from the creature's thrapple. The glove, although covered in blood and gut fluid, was otherwise undamaged.

He stood proud over his kill, his arm dripping. Many had tried to bring down this wild warrior of the woods and failed. The young man bore the name of Livingtoun, and as a reward for his courageous act he was awarded lands stretching from Gullane to North Berwick.

And thus, legend tell us, this is how so the Livingtouns of East Lothian got their land! And this also explains why the head of a boar is to be seen on the family crest, added around the time Saltcoats Castle was built.

Local tradition says the man who brought down the Saltcoats boar was Patrick Livingtoun himself. But the Livingtouns had already been well established in the area for nearly 150 years, so it's possible the tale is older, and the credit was given to Patrick for a deed actually done by one of his ancestors.

But whichever Livingtoun did the deed, evidence of the celebrated event remained in the Saltcoats family for many years. The glove worn and used to choke the poor creature remained in the possession of the family and was actually sold by Lady Saltcoats.

Another item connected to the incident was the helmet said to have been worn by the slayer of the boar. It used to hang in Dirlton Church, but it vanished after being removed while the church underwent some repairs in the late eighteenth century. Someone must know where it is!

The spot by the Peffer Burn where the boar was slain has ever since been known as Livingtoun's Ford.

But as we close this tale, let us spare a moment for the boar. Such animals were dangerous for humans, but no animal is more dangerous to humans than they are to it. If it was indeed Patrick who killed the Saltcoats boar, then that poor animal must have been one of the last wild boars in East Lothian.

Its brutal death is a great tale of bravery and adventure which marked the rise in fortunes of an East Lothian family. But it is also part of the sad story of the decline of Scotland's native wildlife.

35

THE MAUKIN OF DINGLETON

Two hundred years ago, children would pile into Clegham Lizzie's house in Haddington to hear her stories. One of her favourite spooky tales was of the hare of Dingleton, which had been told to her when she was wee. She had no doubt embellished it, but that is the storyteller's prerogative.

The children would huddle around this old storyteller as she set the scene for the story.

'Draw nearer, bairns,' she would say, 'dinnae be feart, weel, no o' me onyway.'

She would begin the tale by asking her usually young audience if they had ever seen a 'maukin'. This was an old Scots word for a hare. Usually the answer was yes, and so she would explore their image of these spectacular creatures. Very occasionally people mistake them for rabbits, but a rabbit is so much smaller and timid. It's the size of a hare that impresses you first. They are often in open fields, and they run incredibly fast, up to 45mph; and they can make incredible leaps into the air.

'Some folk say they hae seen maukins fly,' Lizzie would add, screwing up her eyes and scanning the audience, making a tense atmosphere.

'Anyone seen yin fly?' she would then ask.

Inevitably a younger member of the audience would say they had. Some would laugh, but then Lizzie would add a chill: 'Dinnae laugh at things ye dinnae ken, in case yer laughter is heard.'

'Heard by who?' someone would ask.

She wouldn't answer, but would stare out of the window into the darkness, then return her gaze to the now spooked audience.

So she would tell her tale:

'Hae ye noticed that a maukin will stare at ye? Just like a cat? Weel, there was aince a maukin wha bade close tae Drem. Naebody kent fir sure where it came from. It would just appear in the fields, and some said they even saw it fly.

'Yin day a fairmer wis oot walkin checkin oan his cattle in a field by Dingleton. Then he suddenly saw a maukin as muckle as he'd ever seen. He swore that it was as large as a dug. He stood staring at it and wished he hud brocht his gun.

'He raised his stick and shouted at it, as he wanted tae watch it run. But instead it raised itself on its hind legs and looked at the fairmer. It didnae just look at him though, it stared at him, it wasnae feart. The fairmer walked towards the creature, but it didnae move. It just kept staring at him. Then the fairmer stopped. The maukin's stare sent a shiver doon his spine, something wasnae richt. Sae he ca'd on his collie dugs who came barking.

'This stopped the maukin staring at him, its lang lugs pricking up, then like flash o' lichtening it bolted as the dugs chased it.

'The maukin ran in circles, and leapt ower the dugs, mocking their attempts tae catch it. Then it suddenly headed fir the fairmer's hoose at Dingleton. The dugs chased it but it seemed tae vanish, leaving the hounds sniffing and confused.

'The fairmer wis uneasy, an telt his wife. "That maukin is up tae nae guid, and where did it gang tae?" he wondered. She just looked at him and said naething.

'Ower the next months the fairmer searched wi his dugs fir the maukin's form, but cud find nae sign o' it, or the creature. It seemed tae hae vanished. Maybe it didnae survive the winter, he thocht. But then, the following March, when he'd almaist forgotten aboot it, he saw it agin!

'This time he didnae waste ony time, and set his dugs oan the creature immediately. The maukin was taken by surprise this time,

and the dugs were half upon it afore it stairted tae run. It leapt tae an fro, but the dugs had its measure.

'Aince agin the creature headed fir Dingleton, this time wi the collie dugs richt oan its tail. Yin o' them managed tae bite yin o' the hind legs o' the maukin. The creature let oot a strange cry, then as it approached the hoose it agin vanished oot o' sicht.

'When the fairmer arrived, he saw his dugs sniffing and searching in front o' his hoose, but there was nae sign o' the maukin. It had got away again, but how? It seemed tae huv vanished intae thin air! Where wis it?

'The fairmer was scunnered. How did that maukin get awa frae his dugs after it had been bitten oan the leg?

'He searched wi his dugs but tae nae avail; the maukin hud gotten awa agin!

'Then some of the fairmer's neebours came runnin toward him. "Yer wife, yer wife," they ca'd oot, "she's hurt."

'Sae the fairmer rushed back tae his hoose tae see his wife.

'When he opened the door he got a shock. His guid wife wis lying oan the flair, wi a broken leg, which wis bleeding frae a wound.

'"Whit's happened tae ye?" he asked shocked, as he crouched doon tae tak care o' her. She wis breathing hard, panting as if she'd bin running. Then he looked at her wounded leg. It wis a dug bite!

'"Yer dug bit me," she said. Then he realised.

Lizzie would then pause before finishing the tale, and sweep her transfixed audience with screwed up eyes.

'"Realized whit?" someone would ask, half knowing the answer.

Lizzie would lean forward and draw in her listeners, as she whispered the dark secret.

'"His dugs had been chasing his wife. She had been the maukin. He wis marrit tae a shape shifting witch!"'

36

THE LAST VICAR OF GOLYN

Andro Makghe was the unusual name of the last vicar of Golyn. In the late sixteenth century, and into the early seventeenth, he was a well-kent sight in his parish, now known as Gullane. He was based at the old kirk of St Andrew's and popular legend hands down a most unflattering image of this man.

For a start, we are told that Andro's appearance was one of a man who clearly enjoyed the excesses of pleasure. He had bright red cheeks and reddish bottle nose. He was also very fat, and it was said he would easily gobble down a whole leg of mutton in one meal. His complexion gave away his love for drink, and he consumed copious amounts, especially claret and French wines in general. He also had a reputation for chasing the women, although unsuccessfully.

He had outwardly changed his religion to suit the new times, but the new principles of the Scottish church were not to his liking. He hardly kept this secret as he sang songs, danced and celebrated the old festivals. Despite his portly appearance, the vicar enjoyed the rough and tumble of early football, which was a much rougher game than its modern version.

In fact, based on popular accounts of him, it would be true to say that Andro Makghe's real religion was hedonism!

He was, we are told, disliked by most of his parishioners, for he would exact every penny from them he could, charging for prayers and services whenever possible. And he spent it all on himself. Even his curate was ill fed, skinny and neglected. When they conducted the Sunday service together it looked like a performance by Laurel and Hardy.

Things just went from bad to worse, until one day the vicar was seen plodding to the church, looking dishevelled and hungover. He got to the church and began to prepare for the Sunday service, but became angry as his curate was late. Not only that, the church was also empty, as no one had turned up for Sunday service. Then the curate suddenly appeared.

'Where have you been, you are late,' snorted the vicar. 'And where are the congregation?'

'They are working in their fields and about their business,' replied the curate.

'What? On a Sunday? What godless creatures do I serve here,' cried the vicar.

'It is Monday today,' replied the curate, then added sarcastically, 'the day after Sunday.'

The previous Wednesday had been Ash Wednesday, a day supposed to be set aside for repentance, fasting and abstinence. But the vicar had celebrated it his own way, and had overindulged so much that he had lost a few days, including the Sunday. So as the church had filled up, and the vicar had failed to appear, the curate covered for his boss and told them that he was ill, and conducted the service himself.

But for many of the vicar's parishioners, his failure to turn up for Sunday worship was the last straw. Discontented murmurings developed into discussions amongst some of his flock about how to remove this ill-equipped man of the cloth from his position.

But how to be rid of him? Despite his failings he was still a man of position and connection. In these times, it was not so easy for the common folk to exert influence. By this time the king had managed to introduce bishops to govern the church, and they answered to the king, not the people. Then, an opportunity to take action came when the vicar began to smoke tobacco.

At first the vicar smoked secretly. But soon the curate began to notice the smell that clung to the vicar's vestments. At night, the vicar would stay up, drinking and enjoying a smoke as he prepared for the service. Puffs of smoke would also be seen curling round his head as he walked through his parish. Soon the essence of tobacco smoke began to greet the worshippers as they arrived at church, for as his addiction took hold, the vicar would have a sneaky puff just before conducting the Sunday service.

Eventually the secret was out. The vicar was a smoker!

The king at this time was James VI, and he hated tobacco smoking so much he'd written a treatise called 'A Counterblaste to Tobacco'. In it, the king had written that smoking was a habit 'loathsome to the eye, hateful to the nose, harmful to the brain, and dangerous to the lungs' and that tobacco smoke was 'a black stinking fume' resembling the smoke of hell and only fit for 'diabolical fumigations'!

So, seeing an opportunity, one of the vicar's parishioners galloped to the bishop and informed him that the Vicar of Golyn was smoking. Immediately the vicar was sent for. The king, said the bishop, will not tolerate a smoking clergyman. He must observe this smoking ban or else!

But addiction had a hold on the pleasure-seeking vicar and he couldn't, or wouldn't, give up. So the smell of tobacco smoke continued to cling onto the vicar's vestments and permeate the

vestry. The moment people entered the church they would take deep sniffs and look at each other. 'He's still at it!' they would say.

Soon the inevitable happened. The vicar, we are told, was summoned by the bishop, and due to his breach of this early smoking ban, he finally lost his job.

Yet he seemed unrepentant, declaring: 'I will snuff while I have a nose, and smoke while my stout windpipe blows.' And so, says popular legend, he left, not only his parish, but also the country. Some said he went to France and then Italy where he spent his last years, smoking and drinking to the grave.

And so Andro Makghe remains in folk memory the Smoking Vicar of Golyn. The popular image of him has no doubt been elaborated and coloured by religious point-scoring, but his tale is one of the earliest examples of someone losing their job because they broke a smoking ban!

St Andrew's Kirk was abandoned at much the same time as the smoking vicar's demise. The congregation moved to the newly built kirk at Direlton, opened in 1612. But the wonderfully atmospheric twelfth-century ruins of old St Andrew's remain, and greet you as you enter Gullane by the golf course.

And, it seems, the Smoking Vicar may still be seen around these old ruins. For an old verse tells us:

> Twas said a shape unearthly oft was seen,
> playing at football match on Golyn green.
> Twas said, at dead of night, on Golyn steeple,
> the Vicar smoked, and hallo'd the people.
> Such sights were strange,
> but yet such sights have been.

37

THE MINISTER'S
TATTIE BOGLE

Whittinghame Kirk sits in a quiet corner of East Lothian, as if marooned by a tidal wave of social change. The communities it once served have mostly vanished, swept away by what some call agricultural improvement, and others call the lowland clearances.

It was built in 1722, but almost looks brand new. It is an ancient site, and Christianity is said to have been brought here by St Cuthbert, who built a church nearby in a place still called Kirklands. The present kirk may have been built over the later medieval one. The interior could be described as austere, yet there is a soft atmosphere here. It's a tranquil and beautiful setting.

In the early nineteenth century, the minister of this kirk was the Reverend John Lumsden. As was common, the Reverend Lumsden had a portion of ground called a glebe which was cultivated by the minister for his own use. After planting some potatoes one year, the minister noticed his tattie patch was being raided by crows. On a number of occasions he found himself trying to shoo the birds away, but he quickly came to the conclusion that what was needed was a tattie bogle.

And so Lumsden made a simple frame and searched for suitable clothes to decorate it with. He decided to use an old black suit, still in good condition, but which he hadn't used for some time. He was quite pleased with it, and as a finishing touch he placed a hat on its turnip head. So there it stood, dressed as if for Sunday service, defending the minister's tatties.

But when, sometime later, the minister went to check on his tattie bogle, he was surprised to see that it had changed clothes! Instead of the neat black suit, it now wore a ragged old jacket and a pair of worn dirty trousers. Someone had obviously taken a fancy for the minister's clothes and exchanged them for their own!

That someone was Jock Rattray from Garvald. He had seen the minister's tattie bogle while passing by, and he thought to himself that it seemed a waste of good clothes. They were far superior to his own and, after a sly look to check nobody was about, he ventured carefully onto the tattie patch and began to undress the scarecrow. Another check to ensure no witnesses, then he quickly dropped his breeks, and put on the minister's trousers. They fitted him perfectly, as did the jacket and minister's hat.

The tattie bogle now looked very naked, just two skeletal sticks and a turnip head; that would certainly not scare any crows away. And so Jock dressed it with his old clothes and stood back. 'Aye,' he said to himself, 'that's better, ye'll scare mair craws dressed like that!' And so Jock headed home, the best dressed he had been since he could remember.

Well, not surprisingly Jock's new attire was immediately noticed by all who knew him, but nobody said anything, until his wife saw him.

'Where did ye get thae claes Jock?' she asked suspiciously.

He hesitated for a moment, then replied sheepishly, 'Och, I found them.'

'Ye found them? Dinnae tak me fir a brush, ye dinnae just find braw claes like them, where did ye get them? I hope ye havnae stole them!'

'Naw I didnae, I telt ye I found them,' said Jock, now sounding very defensive.

His wife folded her arms and stared at her husband. She could tell by his body language he was hiding something. 'Sae where did ye find them Jock?' she asked him forcefully.

Jock felt he hadn't told any lies, although perhaps he hadn't told the whole truth. He looked at his wife as she peered at him accusingly with her arms tightly folded.

'I did find them,' he explained, 'a tattie bogle wis wearing them.'

Jock's wife raised her eyebrows and bent her head slightly sideways. She was unconvinced.

'A tattie bogle? Who wad dress a tattie bogle in such fine claes?' she asked.

'Er, weel, it wis the minister's tattie bogle, the minister o' Whittinghame, he's grawin tatties.'

Jock's wife was suddenly horrified: 'Ye stole claes frae the minister! Jock, how cud ye!'

'Naw hen, I telt ye I didnae steal them, I found them on his tattie bogle.'

'But they are still the minister's claes Jock, did ye ask his permission tae tak them?'

Jock bit his lip, looked down at the ground with a guilty lilt and said nothing.

'Weel Jock, did ye ask the minister if ye cud hae his claes?' asked his wife, with arms now unfolded and on her sides.

'Er, naw I didnae, I thocht he wudnae mind.'

'Ye huv committed a sin Jock, a sin.'

Jock managed to recompose his posture and now looked indignant. He mirrored her posture, putting his hands on his hips and launched into a defence of himself.

'No I havnae, it isnae stealing, I just … I just exchanged ma claes wi a tattie bogle, that's no a sin.'

'Aye it is Jock, the Guid Book tells ye sae,' insisted his wife.

Jock was stubborn in his defence. 'Nowhere in the Bible does it say that takin claes frae a tattie bogle is a sin! I just wanted the claes cause they were sae much better than mine, the tattie bogle doesnae even ken it's dressed differently.'

But Jock's wife had Scripture on her side, and she recited from the Ten Commandments, emphasising the last section: 'Thou shall not covet your neighbour's house. You shall not covet your neighbour's wife, or his manservant or maidservant, his ox or donkey, *or anything that belongs to your neighbour.*'

She stared at Jock waiting for his reaction but he just looked at the ground. He hadn't thought his actions were a sin, but now he wasn't so sure. His new clothes now seemed to hang on him guiltily.

His wife wasn't finished, 'It doesnae matter that the minister's claes were oan a tattie bogle, they were the minister's claes and you coveted them and stole them. It's a sin ye've committed, Jock.'

Jock had no choice but to accept the word of God as spoken by his wife. He should have asked the minister, he knew that now.

'A'richt, I'll put the minister's claes back oan the tattie bogle,' Jock said compliantly.

'Naw Jock, ye maun gang tae the minister and tell him it wis ye wha stole his claes. It will not huv passed his notice that his tattie bogle noo has auld claes.'

Jock lowered his head in shame. He felt like a smoke, and reached for his pipe. He realised he'd left it in his jacket pocket with the tattie bogle. That was reason enough for him to return for his clothes.

'Aye, very weel,' said Jock, and he headed back to Whittinghame to confess to the minister. He knew he'd get a hellfire lecture, perhaps some humiliating punishment in the kirk, or even worse, as these were harsh times and folk had been transported for stealing less. If the minister complained to the authorities he might be in real trouble.

He passed the tattie bogle on the way, and noticed that the crows were now completely absent from the field. His pipe was still in the pocket of his old jacket, which flapped in the breeze. He knocked on the minister's door and at first there was no reply. Then the Reverend Lumsden came out.

'Ah, I see now where my old claes have gone, I did wonder,' the minister said.

Jock cleared his throat. 'Aye meenister, I er, weel, saw yer tattie bogle and must admit I did covet its, er, I mean *your* claes, and so I took them. I do reckon the craws are mair feart o yer tattie bogle noo that they are dressed in ma auld claes. But as ma gudewife has telt me, I shud huv cum tae ask ye first.'

'Well they seem tae fit you fine,' observed the minister.

'Aye, they dae, but they werenae mine tae take, and my wife says it wis a sin so she doesnae want me tae wear them.'

Lumsden smiled. 'Your wife is a guid woman, and I'm glad the mystery has been cleared up. But as ye say, the tattie bogle is better dressed fir his purpose now, and I'm satisfied that there has been a guid trade. I cannae judge and forgie ye, only God can dae that, but I cannae see that ony crime or sin has been committed. I just hope ye are happy with the trade as well.'

'Oh aye minister, the claes are braw. Just ane thing tho, I left ma auld clay pipe in ma jacket pocket, may I hae it back?'

'Of course,' said the minister, 'just be careful not to tread on my potatoes.'

'Aye meenister, I'll be careful. Mony thanks fir yer kindness.'

Jock touched his hat, which was once the minister's, but was now rightfully his, and headed for the tattie patch.

He had a spring in his step and a smile on his face. The minister's kindly way of speaking and understanding had been a nice surprise. His clothes were legitimate now and he couldn't wait to tell his wife. She had given him good advice!

He paused when he reached the glebe. He stared at the minister's tattie bogle. It was still flapping in the breeze, but it was no longer wearing his clothes. Someone else had taken Jock's clothes, and replaced them with a jacket and trousers even more worn and dirty than his had been.

And so his pipe was gone as well. Jock sighed to himself and then nodded in understanding. 'Och weel,' he said to the tattie bogle, 'there's ay someone wha's worse off than yersel.'

38

WULLIE'S TOOTH

Wullie lived close to Longniddry, in a small cottage with his wife Jean. He had toothache, the type which causes shooting pain through the gums and entire jaw. 'Yer goanie hae tae get that tooth pu'd oot, Wullie,' said his wife.

Wullie rubbed his jaw. 'I'm no paying guid money for something that can I can dae masel,' he said.

But try as he might, he just couldn't summon the courage to pull the tooth. The moment he tugged at the tooth the pain shot through his gums and he stopped pulling. So he asked his wife if she would help him and pull it out.

'Alricht,' she said, 'you sit doon on the stool and keep yer haunds on yer knees and I'll gie it a richt guid tug.'

Wullie sat on the stool, mouth wide open. His wife bent over him, leaning one of her knees on his thigh, and placing her left hand on his shoulder. She peered into his mouth.

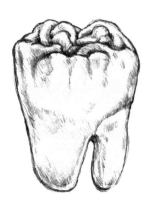

'Aye, I think I can see the bad yin,' she said, tapping it with her finger. Wullie screamed and jumped off the stool, and his wife fell onto the floor.

'Och that wis muckle sair, wit did ye dae that fir?' said Wullie, rubbing his jaw.

His wife picked herself from the floor put her arms by her sides and glared at him.

'Wullie, I maun find the richt tooth first and if ye want me tae help ye've goat tae keep still. I cannae pu' the tooth wi ye jumpin aboot like a chicken oan a hot plate.'

'But it's sair!' protested Wullie.

'I ken it is, but that's the reason it's got tae come oot!' said his wife. Then she paused sympathetically and said, 'Tak a wee bit whisky, that'll help.' She went to the cupboard and took a small jug which contained some homemade whisky. Wullie swished it about his mouth before swallowing it.

'A richt, I'm ready,' he said. He sat on the stool and sat upright, with his hands on his knees. He opened his mouth, closed his eyes, clenched his fists tight and braced himself.

The moment his wife began to tug at the tooth, Wullie leapt up with a scream. Once again, his wife fell onto the floor.

'That's it,' she said. 'I've bin oan the flair twa times noo. Ye can find someyin else tae help ye, I'm no putting up wi this!'

So Wullie sought the help of his best friend, Duncan.

After discussing the issue, Duncan scratched his chin and thought. 'The problem is,' he said, 'the moment onybody touches yer tooth the pain maks ye shriek an ye cannae stay still. Ye've got a rare bad temper at times Wullie, ye ken, I'd be afraid ye'd gie me a punch. Sae gin ye want me tae help, we've got tae find a way tae haud ye doon so ye cannae move when I tak a haud o' yer tooth.'

'Aye, yer right enough Duncan,' said Wullie. 'Whit if ye tie me tae the chair?'

'Naw, that isnae goanie work, cause ye'll still be able tae move yer heid. You'll gie me a heid butt the moment I touch yer tooth.'

The two men thought for a while, then Duncan came up with an idea.

'We could dae it in ma barn, there's a muckle wooden pillar there, I'll tie ye tae it, and then strap yer heid tae it, sae ye cannae move at a'. Then I'll be able tae pu' yer tooth oot wi a pair o' blacksmith's pincers.'

'Braw idea,' said Wullie, and to prepare for it he poured a large amount of whisky into a bottle which he put into his pocket. Then the two friends headed for Duncan's barn.

In no time Wullie was securely tied to the pillar.

'Dinnae footer aboot,' said Wullie, 'just gie it a richt guid tug.'

And so Wullie opened his mouth and Duncan peered inside.

'Aye, I can see the bad yin,' said Duncan.

'Oh wait a minute,' said Wullie, 'I near forgot. In the pocket o' ma jacket there's a wee bottle o' whisky, it's tae help ease the pain.'

Duncan reached into Wullie's pocket and took out the bottle.

'Mebbes I can hae a wee drap tae, ye ken, tae help gie me courage tae pu' yer tooth oot.'

But Wullie was not in a mood to share his whisky.

'It's no ye wha needs the courage, I'm the yin wi the sair tooth. Noo, put the bottle tae ma mooth and I'll drink it all.'

Duncan was suddenly angry at his friend's selfish behaviour. Here he was, helping out, and Wullie wouldn't even share a small drop of his whisky. What kind of friendship was that! Duncan berated his friend's meanness and ingratitude, but Wullie was insistent he needed all the whisky to dull the pain.

Now Wullie was at a great disadvantage in this argument, for he was securely tied up and completely unable to move. So Duncan opened the bottle and jangled it back and fro just under Wullie's nose. He then put the bottle to his own lips and purposefully and slowly took two big gulps.

Wullie saw red and lost his temper, and began to rant and rave at Duncan, calling him names and demanding the whisky. But this had the opposite to the desired effect. Duncan walked casually to the corner of the barn, pulled out a haystack, and placed it a few feet from his ranting friend. Then Duncan purposefully sat on it and made himself comfortable. He took the bottle and took a long inhaling breath, as if he was a whisky connoisseur sniffing its quality. 'This is braw whisky,' he said raising the bottle, and took another gulp.

Wullie struggled like mad to free himself but Duncan had done a good job in securing him to the post. He ranted and raved but could do nothing as Duncan enjoyed the rest of the whisky.

Wullie's anger now turned to utter rage, 'When I get oot o' this I'm goanie ...'

'Yer goanie what?' Duncan interrupted sarcastically, as he stood up and walked back towards his raging friend. Wullie could not even move his head, as it had been securely strapped by the forehead to the pillar. Duncan waved the now empty bottle in front of Wullie.

'Aye,' he said, 'that wis guid whisky,' and he put the bottle back into Wullie's jacket pocket.

Duncan decided it was best to leave his ranting and roaring friend to calm down. He knew what Wullie's temper was like, and there was no way he could pull the tooth while Wullie was in this mood. He would try to bite him! And he certainly wasn't going to untie him just now either, that would be like setting a wild beast free.

So Duncan left the barn and went to his cottage to have a lie down. He intended to return to the barn in a while to see if Wullie had calmed down, as he usually did. But the whisky had gone to his head and so he fell into a deep sleep. He was woken the next morning by a loud knocking on his door. It was Jean, Wullie's wife.

'Is Wullie wi ye?' she asked. 'He didnae come hame last nicht, he'd better no be wi that coo frae the Pans, otherwise he's a deid man.'

Duncan smiled. 'Naw hen, dinnae fash aboot that,' he said, 'but he has spent the nicht wi ma coo in the barn.'

Jean just couldn't stop laughing as she walked home with Wullie; who still had toothache.

39

THE NOBLEMAN'S DAUGHTER AND THE WRAGGLE TAGGLE GYPSY

Jean Hamilton was the daughter of Thomas Hamilton, 1st Earl of Haddington, who bought the Tyninghame Estate in 1628. She was a bonny woman who loved life, and her laughter decorated the old manor house. She would often stroll along the banks of the nearby River Tyne, and it was here in early spring she first met a young man called Sir John Faa of Dunbar.

And so along the banks of the quietly flowing Tyne these two young people fell completely in love with each other. It was more than just sexual passion. By the arrival of summer, she had decided she wanted to marry him and she pledged herself to him.

But this was in an age when noble daughters were expected to marry men approved of, and usually arranged, by their fathers. And when Jean asked her father for permission to marry Johnny Faa of Dunbar, he reacted with rage.

Her father had only recently been created the Earl of Haddington and he planned to use his daughter to make connections with other, more established noble families. This Johnny Faa character was certainly not a suitable husband for this purpose. He was a minor and unimportant knight of low status, and so the earl would not agree to his daughter's desperate pleas to be allowed to marry him.

Instead, Jean's father had chosen the powerful Ayrshire noble John Kennedy, the 6th Earl of Cassilis, to be her husband.

Jean was horrified when she met Cassilis. He was an arrogant, stern and harsh man, and the idea of being with anyone other than her beloved Johnny was just unthinkable. And so, with great courage, she refused to agree to marry this man.

It was a truly heartbreaking situation. Jean pleaded and begged her father but he remained stone-hearted. He forbade her from seeing Johnny, and threatened to hang him if he came anywhere near Tyninghame.

The Earl of Cassilis was also still determined to marry Jean. Her refusal had annoyed him, how dare she turn down an offer from such a rich and powerful man! He felt angered by her refusal but was prepared to wait. Jean's father assured him he would bring his daughter to heel.

But despite her powerless situation, Jean remained determined. She had met a man she truly loved and desired, and she wasn't going to give him up. She didn't care he was of low status. And so she defied her father and continued to meet with her beloved Johnny Faa!

It was dangerous, but the passion they both had for each other made the risk worth it. He would wait for her under a blossoming hawthorn, within sight of the old village of Tyninghame. In summer their love deepened, as they spent long days together by the wooded banks of the Tyne River, witnessed only by a swan.

It was a passionate summer, but inevitably they were seen, and when news of their clandestine meetings reached Jean's father he was enraged. And so was the Earl of Cassilis, who was even more determined to tame this errant woman who dared to defy him.

The Earl of Cassilis searched for Johnny and when they met he insulted and provoked him to draw his sword. Fortunately, friends intervened and a sword fight was avoided, but the earl vowed he would have his revenge. And he did. He used his influence to have Johnny Faa sent away.

A heartbreaking meeting took place on the banks of the Tyne as Johnny explained to Jean that he must leave. It was autumn, and the two lovers were distraught. But he made her a promise:

'I will return to you before the arrival of a second winter, that I vow! And then never part from you again.' In return, Jean promised she would wait for him.

And despite the terrible pressure from her father and Cassilis, she kept her promise. Autumn turned to winter, then spring and summer went. Soon a second winter arrived but there was still no sign of her lover.

Jean was in emotional turmoil. Where was he? Why hadn't he returned as he'd promised? Then she got word that he was in Spain. Soon afterwards, the Earl of Cassilis arrived with a satisfied smile on his face. He showed her a letter from the ambassador of Spain. With trembling hands, she read it.

Jean was devastated. The letter said a man called Sir John Faa of Dunbar had been murdered in Madrid. She collapsed in grief.

Now she was heartbroken, and no longer cared what happened to her, so she gave in and agreed to marry Cassilis.

The marriage celebration took place at Tyninghame Manor. No expense was spared, it was a lavish party, but it was a travesty. Jean sat bleary eyed and unhappy, while her stern and unemotional husband seemed unconcerned by his bride's miserable state. Jean's father was just as cold-hearted. He cared little for his daughter's unhappiness, he was satisfied that his plans to elevate his family status had been achieved. He was angry that his daughter wasn't hiding her unhappiness, she looked miserable and then, emotionally exhausted, she fainted before her wedding night.

The following day, a heartbroken and defeated Jean was taken by her husband to his home at Cassilis in Ayrshire, on the banks of the Doon River. The old castle was large and Jean was lonely and neglected. She bore Cassilis three children, but he had no other interest in her. He had no love for Jean, she was just a trophy wife to him. He sometimes showed her off at formal functions, but most of the time she was left alone in the castle with unfriendly servants. Her husband was heavily involved in both church and state affairs and was away most of the time, wrapped up in his own self-importance.

After four years of this miserable existence, Jean was a shadow of her former self. Life no longer seemed to have any meaning. She'd forgotten how to laugh. Not a day went by without her thinking of her beloved Johnny Faa.

Then one day, while walking on the battlements of the castle, she saw a group of armed gypsies approaching. Her husband, as usual, was away on business, so she ordered the castle gates locked, but she remained curious and watched as they arrived below the castle's walls. They were wonderfully dressed and began to play and sing to her.

The man who was the leader moved closer to the wall, looked up at Jean and sang directly to her. Suddenly she recognised his voice.

'No, no, it can't be,' she thought.

Then Jean's legs almost gave way and her heart leapt. Waves of emotion convulsed her body, she wanted to cry out but her voice was dry.

It was her Johnny!

She vanished from the battlements and tore down the spiral stairs, then rushed through the gates. She ran towards Johnny, her tears of joy streaming from her face, and threw herself at him.

A scream of utter joy came from her inner soul as she wrapped herself around the man she loved. The other gypsies continued singing as she showered Johnny with tear-stained kisses.

But Johnny also had some explaining to do!

He had been caught up in the inquisition in Madrid, and thrown into prison. He had been unable to send word of his plight. He had feared he would die there. Every day that went by he thought of Jean. He was desperate to escape, but it was not possible. However, after over five years he eventually managed to gain his freedom, and came with all the speed he could back to Scotland.

'You can imagine the darkness that descended on me when I was told you had married Cassilis,' said Johnny. 'I blamed myself, since I had broken my promise to return within a year. But then I was told of your unhappiness and I resolved to come and see if you still loved me as I do you.'

He then explained, 'I came as a gypsy to disguise myself, for I wish to take you away.' He hesitated, then continued, 'That is, if you will come with me. We will have to live as fugitives. The moors, the hillsides and forests will be our home. We will live as gypsies.'

'Come away with you and live a gypsy life?' said Jean. 'I am the wife of a great noble and daughter of another. You ask me to give up my great home, my comforts, my titles and status, my feathered bed for a roaming gypsy life sleeping on the heather?'

Johnny bowed his head, desperately disappointed, but nodding in understanding.

'Foolish man!' said Jean. 'Of course I will come with you! These walls are a prison, and what use do I have of a feather mattress without love, when the soft heather on the moor awaits? As long as I am with you! That is all that matters.'

She mounted his horse with him, and clasped her arms around his chest. Then she rode away with her lover and the gypsies.

The old folk song called 'The Wraggle Taggle Gypsies o!' celebrates this moment:

> What care I for my house and my land?
> What care I for my money, O?
> What care I for my new wedded lord?
> I'm off with the wraggle taggle gypsies, O!
>
> What care I for a goose-feather bed?
> With the sheet turned down so bravely, O!
> For to-night I shall sleep in a cold open field,
> Along with the wraggle taggle gypsies, O!'

But what happened next? Did they live happily ever after?

Well, the oldest version of the ballad suggests they did. But go to Ayrshire and the most popular version of the story there is the one which ends with the Earl of Cassilis hanging all the gypsies on the Dule Tree, including Johnny Faa, in front of his castle, then banishing Jean to Maybole Castle for the rest of her life. It is a tale in which you can choose the ending, for while historians will question the truth of its origins, the storyteller will point to the deeper truth of the story's message: that love can conquer all.

40

THE LONELY GRAVES
OF GILCHRISTON

William Skirvin was the tenant farmer of Gilchriston in the early seventeenth century. He was well respected and liked, and was known locally as the Gudeman of Gilchriston. He lived there with his wife and daughter, plus two serving women and a ploughman.

William Skirvin's daughter was called Ellen. She was an o nly child by the time she had reached adolescence, and was deeply loved. By the summer of 1645, she had blossomed into a beautiful young woman.

She would often take an evening walk by the riverbank and in the nearby woods, to pick flowers and berries or enjoy the birdsong. One evening, she set off 'doon the burn' as the trees were casting long shadows at the end of the day. But before she returned the weather changed dramatically, and she found herself caught in a ferocious thunderstorm, with lightning searing the sky.

Although her home was not far away, she was not clothed for such weather and so she sought shelter in a woodman's hut. The rain was pelting down, and then suddenly a streak of lightning split a tree standing nearby. It was quite scary, and she decided to say where she was until the storm passed.

Suddenly a young man appeared at the door. He had also been caught in the storm and was likewise seeking shelter. Needless to say, he was a bit taken aback by the sight of a pretty young woman sitting in this hut in the middle of the wood.

He hesitated for a moment, not wanting to alarm her. There was an awkward moment and then the young man spoke.

'Please forgie me, I mean no tae intrude, but the weather ootside is the deil's ain.'

Ellen smiled, and reassured the young man he was welcome, so he entered the hut and sat a respectable distance away from her.

The storm lasted for another ten bone-crunchingly awkward minutes. Two young people in a hut together in a wood! What scandal if they were found!

The young man did his best to remain formal and polite, but he could not take his eyes off her. He found her extremely attractive, and her shyness and apparent innocence just increased his interest.

And so to break an awkward silence in their conversation, he offered to accompany her home.

She smiled, but politely declined. 'Your goodness, sire, deserves my respect, but there is nae need tae put yersel tae ony trouble, as I can wait here till the storm is abated. I am the daughter o' William Skirvin o' Gilchriston, and ma hame is but a few minutes' walk frae here.'

A broad grin decorated the young man's face. 'I am delighted tae hear that ye are the daughter o' my father's respected tenant!' He then introduced himself. He was Henry, the son of the laird, the local landowner.

Then the storm broke, the rain stopped and Henry saw his opportunity.

'I will do masel the pleasure o' paying a visit tae Mr Skirvin as the companion o' his bonny daughter, who I have met sae unexpectedly!' Ellen could hardly refuse, and so the two young people emerged from the hut and took the short walk to the farmstead at Gilchriston.

When they arrived, they were greeted by Ellen's mother. When she first saw her daughter walking up the slope in the company of a young man she was shocked. But as soon as the young man introduced himself and she realised he was a nobleman's son, her demeanour changed. Henry was invited into the house, where William personally thanked Henry for his assistance to his daughter.

But then the storm returned. Rain came down in buckets and so Henry was invited to stay and eat.

The serving girls prepared the meal, and just before the meal was ready the ploughman arrived. His name was Andrew Harrowlea, a young man the same age as Henry. Normally the serving girls and Andrew would eat with the Skirvin family, but today they had a distinguished guest so William asked the servants to eat at the back of the house on this occasion.

Ellen arrived, having changed her droukit clothes. Her mother couldn't but notice the expression on Henry's face as Ellen sat opposite the smitten young man. It was an exciting event for the Skirvins. Not every day did they have a noble visitor sitting at their old oak table!

Ellen's mother could hardly stop speaking. 'Little did I think when oor bairn gaed doon the burn i' the gloaming tae gaither slaes, or look fir cushie-doos' nests i' the wood, that she was tae sune hame wi sic a …' she was just about to say 'braw wooer', but

a raised eyebrow from Ellen quickly made her realise she was being presumptuous, and so just in time she changed words and said, '... er, wi sic a guest as you, maister Henry.'

It was agony for Henry. He couldn't read Ellen's feelings. He nodded politely as her mother blethered away, but Ellen herself said almost nothing. But every now and then she looked at him from across the table, and graced the looks with a faintly discernible smile. They sent shockwaves of desire through his body, but was he misreading her interest?

By the meal's end, the storm had vanished and a cool and calm night hung outside. Ellen's father William offered to accompany Henry to the gate, and so the young man made his polite farewell. Andrew the ploughman accompanied them. Henry thanked William for his kind hospitality, and the young nobleman made his way home.

Andrew and William looked at each other; they both knew fine well what Henry's intentions were, but neither said anything.

That night Ellen could barely sleep. She had butterflies in her stomach and an irremovable smile on her face. The next day, she found herself walking once again by the riverside. She was heading for the woodman's hut. She wasn't sure why, but as she approached the hut waves of anticipation overtook her. Nothing had been arranged, but somehow she hoped she might find Henry there.

And she did! They both knew why they had returned, but for Ellen this was unknown emotional ground, and she wasn't sure how to act. But Henry did. He kissed her, and so began Ellen's first love affair.

Henry was impatient and so was Ellen, and so they would meet secretly by their trysting tree in a lonely corner of the dell. It was a passionate and deeply felt love affair, as all first loves are.

But this was 1645, a time of great turmoil. Civil war was raging in the country, with supporters and opponents of King Charles I tearing the country apart. The Royalist forces of Montrose were now in the lowlands, and Henry was called to join his father's regiment to fight against Montrose.

And so on an August day, after they had met at the trysting tree, Henry broke the news to Ellen.

'I maun gang wi ma faither and gain glory in battle,' said Henry excitedly, 'but on ma return I will ask yer faither fir yer haund!'

Ellen's response was not what he expected. She fell to her knees. 'There is nae longer happiness fir me oan this earth, for I ken in ma heart that thou will fall in battle and be lost tae me forever.'

'Naw bonny lass, I will return a hero!' said Henry. Ellen then composed herself and put on a brave face for her excited and naive lover. They said their farewells, but as she watched him leave she leant against the tree and was overtaken by anxiety.

Three days later, Ellen received the news that Henry had been killed at the Battle of Kilsyth. The news was brought by a returning soldier, who also brought something else. The disruption and deprivations caused by the civil war, combined with the movement of people across the country, had helped spread the plague.

The folk of Edinburgh were dying like flies in the worst outbreak of the disease it was ever to suffer. But until now, the plague had not visited this quiet corner of East Lothian.

Ellen was the first to succumb to its deadly and cruel grip. The rest of the parish was as yet plague-free, so William could not venture beyond Gilchriston to bury his daughter, and no one would come near them, not even the minister.

And so William, with the help of Andrew his ploughman, prepared a grave for his beloved Ellen, close to the river where she used to go walking. Both men wept as William read from the Bible. The outside world had come to this quiet corner with a vengeance. William's wife lay in the house dying also, as well as the two female servants. All three were likewise soon afterwards buried by William and Andrew.

Then William himself got sick. His ploughman helped him prepare his own grave, and the next day the faithful Andrew Harrowlea laid his master to rest next to his family.

A visit to these lonely graves is a powerful experience. The river still runs nearby and trees still grace this lovely wee valley. Although this is a tale with a sad ending, it reminds us that everything comes to an end, and sometimes sooner than we expect.

But they were happy in life, and instead of lying unnoticed in an old graveyard, William Skirvin and his family rest together in the land they once tilled, and amongst the trees where Ellen in life found deeply felt romantic love. Few plague victims had such a personal and special place to rest.

And there is a wee twist to this tale. The ploughman, Andrew Harrowlea, loved Ellen also. It is from him we get the story. He watched silently, no doubt in some emotional pain, as the woman he loved fell for another. He watched to keep her safe, and when he laid her to rest he was as distraught as William her father was.

It is said it was he who later erected the stones, which likely had other inscriptions, now too worn to identify. It is said also that a later descendant of the Skirvins then erected the iron fence around the graves to keep them safe.

The inscription is almost unreadable now, but it says: 'Heir Lyes William Skirvin, Who Desicit the 24 of Ivinne, 1645'. Next to William's grave is that of Katrin Wilson, very likely his beloved wife.

The graves lie close to the Birns water, where trees still hang over the river.

41

'TO HERDMANSTON!'

On a bend in the River Tyne, a mile or so downriver from Pencaitland, there sits an ancient chapel in which generations of the Sinclairs of Herdmanston rest. The chapel has its origins in the thirteenth century, although it was restored in 1840.

The castle and mansion which used to stand beside the chapel have now gone, and so this ancient burial place of one of East Lothian's oldest noble lines seems strangely marooned atop a ridge and surrounded by fields of grazing cows. The Sinclair connection goes back to 1162, when Henry De St Clair was granted a charter to Herdmanston.

It was a descendant, Sir William St Clair (not to be confused with the namesake from Roslyn) who fought with Robert the

Bruce at Bannockburn. Such was his bravery at that battle that The Bruce gave him an engraved sword with the words in Latin: 'The king gave me, Sinclair carries me'.

The following tale, however, is about a later Sir William Sinclair or, to be more precise, about his two nieces, Marion and Margaret; two young and beautiful noblewomen.

The tale begins in 1472, with the death of the young women's father, John St Clair of Herdmanston. He had also held the estates of Kimmerghame and Polwarth in the Borders and so left these estates to his daughters, Marion inheriting Kimmerghame and her sister Margaret got Polwarth. They were both sizeable and desirable inheritances. Herdmanston went to John's brother, another William St Clair.

All well and fair you might think, except William was not so satisfied. He had an eye on his nieces' estates. He was sly at first, putting ideas into their heads that they would be better off allowing him to be guardian of their land, that he could run their estates better. But the young women were having none of this. They were confident of their own abilities and besides, they hoped soon to marry, for they both had young suitors, George and Patrick Hume of Wedderburn, who would take on the responsibilities of running the estate. Marion desired Sir George while Margaret had eyes for Sir Patrick. They were both, it seems, determined to marry the brothers, despite their uncle's opposition.

So William invited his two nieces to his castle at Hermanston for a party, at which an array of alternative suitors would be present. It would be a veritable Magaluf by the Tyne! If, after meeting all these young and suitable potential husbands, they still wanted to marry Patrick and George, then he would accept this.

But Margaret, the younger sister, was suspicious. She had faint memories of an overheard conversation between her mother and father in which they talked of her uncle as untrustworthy. Perhaps that is why their uncle was not appointed as guardian of their estates, as tradition would have expected.

But Marion argued that they should be more conciliatory. 'Come sister, let us go and indulge our uncle's desire to sway us, and perhaps when he sees our hearts and minds are set he will finally accept our decision.'

And so the two young women made their way to their uncle's castle at Herdmanston, accompanied by only one servant each.

Their uncle gave them a hearty welcome as they arrived at the castle gate, but the moment the doors closed behind them, his face changed. There were no guests, no party atmosphere. Instead, their now grim-faced uncle lectured them on their disrespect of his wishes, and that as women they should listen to the advice of their male superior.

The two sisters huddled together, but refused to agree to sign control of their estates over to him.

'Very well,' he said, 'you will languish here until you realise there is no other course.'

After two days in the dank prison, the door opened and their uncle entered. He smirked as he enquired as to their comfort and told them that they could gain their freedom if they married two cousins, over whom he had control. He gave them eight days to consider his proposal, with the clear threat that if they declined, then it would be a matter of great regret for them.

The sisters locked arms and Margaret wanted to say something, but her sister touched her arms. 'Hush sister, leave alone, we are in no position to argue.'

The door closed and dank semi-darkness descended again. Marion now wept. She felt such guilt. She should have listened to her sister's warnings and now blamed herself for their awful predicament. But Margaret comforted her.

'When George and Patrick hear of this they will come rescue us,' she said.

'But no one knows we are here,' replied Marion despondently.

'We will find a way to alert them,' was her sister's confident reply.

But how?

Well, here is where the tale takes a romantic twist. Just as the eighth day was approaching, the sisters heard the sound of singing and musical instruments. It was a group of gypsies, led by none other than Johnny Faa himself, the self-styled 'King of the Gypsies'.

The sisters seized the moment and called out desperately through the barred, narrow slit window that was their only source of daylight.

'Our uncle holds us here against our will, please will you tell Patrick and George Wedderburn, for they will surely come to rescue us.'

Johnny Faa agreed with the grace of a gypsy king. 'With haste, maidens, I will spare not my pony.'

And so he galloped his faithful pony over the Lammermuirs to Wedderburn Castle. The sight of Johnny Faa at the gate in such a state roused much alarm. Patrick Hume met the gypsy with great suspicion, and insultingly called him nothing but a king of gaberlunzie men.

But Johnny then conveyed his message. 'The maiden who loves you is imprisoned in her uncle's castle at Herdmanston, along with her sister. They will not survive long, for their uncle has an eye on their estates.'

Sir Patrick was stung into action. He apologised for his rude behaviour, and quickly informed his brother George. Within hours they had over 100 men-at-arms!

'To Herdmanston!' was their cry, and the heavily armed force galloped over the Lammermuirs into East Lothian, led by the two brothers.

It was daybreak when they arrived at Herdmanston. The sound of their approach was heard by the sisters, who could just glimpse the sight of their rescuers through their narrow window. The banner of the Humes was fluttering in the wind! The sisters knew their lovers had come to rescue them!

But Sir William had a force of his own. He summoned fifty men, and sent messengers for further aid. His men rushed out of the gates and met the brothers' force head-on. Battle ensued, the noise of bones splitting, men and horses dying filled the air. Margaret and Marion strained to see, but all was confusion.

Then William Sinclair's neighbours arrived with more men, and the tide turned in his favour. The Hume brothers fought gallantly but they were now outnumbered. All seemed lost for them, until suddenly a new force arrived. It was Johnny Faa, with a contingent of gypsy warriors.

Now the battle drew to a quick close. Sinclair's forces fled, and Sir William found himself at the end of Sir Patrick Hume's sword, begging for mercy.

Mercy was given, but the two brothers rushed into the castle and rescued the women they loved. The battle had lasted all day, and so the journey back to Wedderburn was by moonlight.

Within a few weeks, the sisters were married to the brothers; Margaret married Sir Patrick, and Marion married his brother Sir George. They danced around a thorn tree at Polwarth Green to the music of the gypsies, and I suppose the double wedding is a tale in itself.

42

MUSSELBURGH'S FAMOUS FISHWIFE

Maggie Dickson was a Musselburgh fishwife and lived in the eighteenth century. She was poor, and history rarely records the life of people such as Maggie. But her husband deserted her after the birth of her second child, and this would change Maggie's life forever.

Maggie was in a desperate situation. She had friends and relatives who helped her, but with her husband gone she was struggling. Then she heard her husband was working in Newcastle, and so she decided to visit an aunt who lived there and see if she could find her husband. It would be a long journey, but she wanted to know why he had left. Perhaps she could find her husband and return later. Life now seemed so unsure, she had to try. So she left her children in the care of relatives and set off.

Maggie never made it to Newcastle. When she arrived in the border town of Kelso she was penniless, so she looked for work. She managed to get a job in an inn near to the town. It didn't pay much, but at least she now had a place to stay and could save a little.

The son of the inn's owner was called William Bell, and he took a real fancy to Maggie. At first she tried to resist his advances, but eventually they became lovers. Maybe she loved him, maybe she was just lonely or afraid she'd lose her job.

Then one day, Maggie felt dizzy.

'Ye alricht hen?' asked the landlady.

'Aye fine,' replied Maggie. But she wasn't.

Later that day she felt sick. Maggie knew what it was. She was pregnant. Within a few weeks, her swelling tummy confirmed what she already knew. She lay in bed with a panic. She was still technically married. Her baby was obviously not her husband's. What shame would this bring on her? But not only that. This was the early eighteenth century. Women in her condition were publicly humiliated, heads shaven and forced to stand outside the church chained to the wall in a metal collar called the jougs, like a dog on Sundays, so everyone would know of her sin.

So, in her terror, she concealed her pregnancy. She would work for as long as possible, then leave for Newcastle. She thought about telling William, but she was still married, so what could he do? She didn't want to bring shame on him as well. She felt so alone.

As her tummy grew she had to strap it tightly, so the telltale bump wasn't visible. Then one day she felt the baby arriving. She had to give birth secretly, muffling her cries. But the baby was early, and it didn't survive. She cradled her lifeless child in her arms for a while. But now she must find a way to hide the baby's body. She was in terrible danger if discovered.

So, in the twilight she walked down to the River Tweed. It flowed fast and deep past the town, and it would take her child out to sea. But as she stood on the banks of the river, she couldn't do it. And so she gently and lovingly wrapped the child in her shawl and hid it under a nearby bush. Perhaps she could find a way to give her child a proper burial.

But fate was not to allow this. The child was discovered wrapped in her shawl, and she was arrested and charged under the 1690 Concealment of Pregnancy Act. This was a harsh law designed to prevent women from concealing their pregnancy. Many women who become pregnant out of wedlock were terrified of the punishment and shame that would be heaped upon them, so they would conceal their pregnancy. But they took a huge risk, as this law stated that if a woman concealed her pregnancy and gave birth without assistance, the death of the child would be treated as murder, even if no evidence of murder existed.

Maggie languished in the dark prison of Edinburgh's Tollbooth. She was visited by friends and relatives, but she was poor and the law had already hanged women in her situation. During her trial, she appealed for leniency. She explained that she had been deserted by her husband and was in a desperate situation. That she loved her child, which is why she couldn't bring herself to cast it into the river.

It was no good. The law was clear. She had concealed her pregnancy, given birth in secret and her child did not survive. The only punishment according to law was execution.

'Ye will be taken doon tae the tollbooth,' said the judge after the guilty verdict was pronounced, 'and there ye will bide till the time o' yer execution, tae be carrit oot on 2nd September o' this year, 1724, when ye will be hangit by yer neck till ye be deid.' Some of Maggie's friends started to cry in the court and Maggie broke down as they led her away.

The execution was very soon, and now Maggie had another terror: dissection on the surgeon's table. For the bodies of those convicted to murder were usually handed to the college of surgeons for dissection. It was an extra punishment, as many people then believed that the whole body was needed for the time of the second coming.

'They'll cut you up,' said one of the prison warders to Maggie. 'Slice yer pretty face and yer body. Ye will be unrecognisable to God.' Her weeping solicited no compassion. 'Dinnae greet, ye should've thocht o' that afore ye committed yer sin.'

But Maggie had friends. She was liked by many in Musselburgh and all could see the injustice of her fate. And so they got organised and raised money for a coffin. They got word to Maggie. They would be there. They would stand at the front of the crowd. They would pray for her and try to keep her strong. And afterwards they would take her body and keep it secure in the coffin. They would not allow anyone to take her to the medical school. They would bury her at Inveresk.

'If we hae tae fecht fir ye Maggie, we will,' said one of her friends. Maggie was partly reassured and moved by the loyalty and help of her friends.

Dawn of 2 September 1724 arrived. Maggie was led from the Tolbooth on the Royal Mile to the Grassmarket, where a large scaffold had been erected. There was a huge crowd of people, but at the front, as promised, were her friends with a coffin. Maggie was allowed a few precious moments to say goodbye to them.

She mounted the scaffold. Her face was pale and her legs trembled. She whispered a final goodbye to her friends and was then ordered to climb the ladder. He hands were tied behind her back, the noose was placed around her neck and tightened. Her head felt dizzy and then the hangman pushed her off, and she began to choke as the rope burned into her neck as she swung to and fro.

Then she entered a darkness and her legs stopped kicking.

A hush swept over the crowd as they watched Maggie choke on the rope. Her legs twitched and kicked for a moment, but soon her body hung lifeless. She remained for the required time and then the hangman pulled her by the legs to extinguish any life that may be left in her.

The doctor examined her. 'Aye, she's deid,' he said. It was a cursory examination, as he was keen to join the magistrates for the customary meal taken by officials after a hanging. And finally, Maggie's body was taken down.

Her friends now sprang into action, quickly placing her body in the coffin, then nailing the lid down and standing guard against any attempt to take her body.

But then, as the crowd began to disperse and Maggie's friends were placing the coffin on a cart, a group of apprentice surgeons from the college emerged. They had hired heavies with them. Maggie's friends had feared this would happen, but they were ready.

A fight ensued, but the young surgeons and their hired thugs had no idea what they were up against. Many of Maggie's friends were fishwives. They were used to carrying heavy creels of fish for miles and had muscles to match. They stood around their friend's coffin and defended it.

The scuffle didn't last long. These men were no match against fishwives! The coffin was slightly damaged by a hammer, but the surgeons were driven off with bloody noses and cries of derision. The coffin was then taken quickly along the Cowgate on the way to Inveresk. Maggie's friends had kept their promise to keep her safe from the dissection table.

The cart went by way of Duddingston. The man driving the cart was thirsty, and so a stop was made at an inn at Peppermill. As he and some of Maggie's friends and family had a drink, the strange sight of the coffin parked outside drew some attention.

Two men passing by noticed the damage on the coffin. They were joiners, so were casting a professional eye over it when one of them suddenly froze.

'Ye hear that, it's coming frae inside the coffin!' he said.

The two men listened. Sure enough, faint sounds were coming from inside. A groaning noise. They looked at each other in disbelief, then ran into the inn.

'Wha's is the coffin oot there?' they cried. 'There's groanin comin frae it!'

'Och awa wi ye,' said the cart owner, refusing to believe it, 'yer unco fou an hearin things.'

But the two men insisted. 'I'm tellin ye,' said one, 'there's groaning comin frae inside that coffin!'

Maggie's friends and family went out to investigate. A small crowd had assembled around them.

'I cannae hear onything,' the carter said.

'I'm telling ye, there wis groaning,' insisted one of the joiners.

'Ye cannae pit Maggie in the groond no kenning wit that noise is,' said a fishwife friend of Maggie's.

There was eventually agreement that the coffin should be opened, but no one wanted to be the one to do it. Eventually, one brave soul agreed and began to remove the nails from the lid and open the coffin. He peered inside. There lay Maggie's body.

Then an arm moved, and a groan was heard. You couldn't see the terrified onlookers for dust, as they ran away as fast as they could!

But there was one man who didn't flee. His name was Peter Purdie. He looked at Maggie. Could it be possible she was really alive? Or was this just the twitching of a corpse, the groans a result of air being released from the lungs? He had seen such things before. He was a phlebotomist, someone who took blood from people to help cure them. He decided to bleed her to discover if she was alive.

He made a small cut in a vein, and blood streamed out. Maggie stirred again. She was alive!

'She's alive, she's alive, in God's name she's alive!' Peter cried out.

Courage returned to the onlookers and suddenly people began to help. Blankets were brought, and she was carefully lifted onto the cart. And so, followed by a crowd, Maggie was carefully driven to Musselburgh.

When they arrived, the news that Maggie was alive had already spread. Few believed it at first but everyone wanted to find out. There was a danger that things could get out of hand. So a local official ordered that, in the meantime, Maggie should be sent to her brother's house. His name was James Dickson, and he had been preparing for his sister's wake!

Maggie lay in her brother's house as a stream of visitors arrived. But her brother had to keep them at bay. She was alive, but only just. He allowed the minister for Inveresk to see her, and some of her close friends.

But Maggie was barely clinging onto life. Her friends and family wept and prayed by her bedside. Every now and then she cried out, but seemed only half alive.

But within two days she began to recover. She asked for whisky and complained of a sore neck! Only a few days after her 'execution', she attended church. She was by now a local celebrity, and the minister had to escort her from the building at the end of the service as people attempted to see her.

But soon the gossip and legal arguments began. She had been sentenced to hang by the neck until she was dead, but she was now most definitely alive. How could that be? Was she a witch? Was the hanging botched, and if so should she be hanged again?

She was imprisoned and questioned, as were all involved, including the doctor who had pronounced her dead. He insisted that he could not have been wrong. His evidence was accepted, but then how could she now be alive and what was to be done?

The verdict on Maggie's fate was finally agreed upon by magistrates and church figures. Since the doctor had confirmed she was dead, the execution had been fully carried out according to law. The fact she was now alive could only be an act of God, and no man had the right to reverse God's will. Maggie was free and lived for another forty years!

And so the rest of her life became another story, and she was forever after known by her popular nickname: Half-Hangit Maggie!

GLOSSARY

aboot	about	cushie-doo	wood-pigeon
agin	again	dae	do
aifter	after	deid	dead
ails	troubles	deil	devil
ain	own	didnae	didn't
aince	once	dinnae	don't
alang	along	doon	down
almichty	almighty	droukit	wet
alricht	alright	een	eyes
an	and	fairmer	farmer
ane	one	faither	father
aroond	around	fash	bother
atween	between	fecht	fight
awa	away	fir	for
ay	always	flair	floor
aye	yes	forgie	forgive
bairn	child	fou	full/drunk
bides	lives	frae	from
braw	good	gaberlunzie	beggar
bricht	bright	gaed	went
brocht	brought	gang	go
cairt	cart	gangin	going
cannae	can't	ghaist	ghost
claes	clothes	gied	gave
cokenny	cockenzie	gien	given
commandit	commanded	groond	ground
cowerit	cowered	guid	good

hae	have	niver	never
hale	whole	noo	now
hairted	hearted	o'	of
hame	home	oan	on
haud	hold	ony	any
haund	hand	onymair	anymore
heid	head	onything	anything
hen	dear	oorsels	ourselves
hoose	house	oot	out
hud	hold	ower	over
hunner/s	hundred/s	pairt	part
huv	have	poonds	pounds
intae	into	sae	so
ither	other	sair	sore
jaicket	jacket	sicht	sight
ken	know	sleekit	sneaky
kirk	church	snell	quick
lang	long	stairted	started
licht	light	stane	stone
ma	my	strang	strong
maist	most	tae	too
maister	master	tak	take
mak	make	telt	told
marrit	married	thae	those
masel	myself	thochts	thoughts
maun	must	toon	town
mebbe	maybe	twa	two
meenister	minister	unco	extremely
mither	mother	wee	small
moose	mouse	weel	well
muckle	big	whit	what
na	no	wi	with
naethin	nothing	wis	was
naw	no	wud	would
neebours	neighbours	ye	you
nicht	night		

A NOTE ON THE SOURCES

Folk tales come from many sources, many not of which were not written down. However, the following published sources have been used for some of the stories:

St Baldred of the Bass: A Pictish Legend by James Miller, 1824;
Popular Rhymes of Scotland by Robert Chambers, 1870;
Reminiscences of the Royal Burgh of Haddington and Old East Lothian Agriculturalists by Martine John, 1883;
Prestonpans: Scotland's last Salt Works by Alex Hamilton and Margaret Nisbet, 1976;
Philip Stanneld, the Parricide and Other Tales by George Tait, 1838.

Many of the stories have emerged from old ballads, chapbooks, old manuscripts, chronicles, newspaper cuttings, fragments of rhyme and, in particular, the oral tradition. Sir Walter Scott's writings are in themselves a treasure trove for traditional tales, and his indelible fingerprints are in this book too.

Readers of my column 'Tim's Tales' in the East Lothian Courier have been a constant source and motivation for my quest for stories, and for that I am very grateful.

All the stories are deeply flavoured with my own imagination and poetic licence, and as such they are now stories you are free to share with others. That, after all, is the spirit of the storytelling tradition.

Happy Storytelling!

Scottish Storytelling Forum

The Scottish Storytelling Centre is delighted to be associated with the *Folk Tales* series developed by The History Press. Its talented storytellers continue the Scottish tradition, revealing the regional riches of Scotland in these volumes. These include the different environments, languages and cultures encompassed in our big wee country. The Scottish Storytelling Centre provides a base and communications point for the national storytelling network, along with national networks for Traditional Music and Song and Traditions of Dance, all under the umbrella of TRACS (Traditional Arts and Culture Scotland). See www. scottishstorytellingcentre.co.uk for further information. The Traditional Arts community of Scotland is also delighted to be working with all the nations and regions of Great Britain and Ireland through the *Folk Tales* series.